So You've Been Publicly Shamed

Also by Jon Ronson

Jon Ronson ←

So You've Been Publicly Shamed

RIVERHEAD BOOKS   A MEMBER OF PENGUIN GROUP (USA)   NEW YORK   2015

RIVERHEAD BOOKS
Published by the Penguin Group
Penguin Group (USA) LLC
375 Hudson Street
New York, New York 10014

USA · Canada · UK · Ireland · Australia
New Zealand · India · South Africa · China

penguin.com
A Penguin Random House Company

Library of Congress Cataloging-in-Publication Data

Ronson, Jon, date.
   So you've been publicly shamed / Jon Ronson.
      p.   cm.
ISBN 978-1-59448-713-2
1. Social control.   2. Shame.   3. Interpersonal relations.   I. Title.
HM661.R66   2015   2014038382
152.4'4—dc23

Printed in the United States of America
10 9 8 7 6 5 4 3

BOOK DESIGN BY MEIGHAN CAVANAUGH

For Elaine

Contents

So You've Been Publicly Shamed

One

Braveheart

This story begins in early January 2012, when I noticed that another Jon Ronson had started posting on Twitter. His photograph was a photograph of my face. His Twitter name was @Jon_Ronson. His most recent tweet, which appeared as I stared in surprise at his timeline, read: "Going home. Gotta get the recipe for a huge plate of guarana and mussel in a bap with mayonnaise :D #yummy."

"Who are you?" I tweeted him.

"Watching #Seinfeld. I would love a big plate of celeriac, grouper and sour cream kebab with lemongrass. #foodie," he tweeted.

I didn't know what to do.

The next morning I checked @Jon_Ronson's timeline before I checked my own. In the night he had tweeted, "I'm dreaming something about #time and #cock."

He had twenty followers. Some were people I knew from real life, who were probably wondering why I'd suddenly become so passionate about fusion cooking and candid about dreaming about cock.

I did some digging. I discovered that a young researcher, formerly of Warwick University, called Luke Robert Mason had a few weeks earlier posted a comment on the *Guardian* site. It was in response to a short video I had made about spambots. "We've built Jon his very own infomorph," he wrote. "You can follow him on Twitter here: @Jon_Ronson."

Oh, so it's some kind of spambot, I thought. *Okay. This will be fine. Luke Robert Mason must have thought I would like the spambot. When he finds out that I don't, he'll remove it.*

So I tweeted him: "Hi!! Will you take down your spambot please?"

Ten minutes passed. Then he replied, "We prefer the term *infomorph.*"

I frowned. "But it's taken my identity," I wrote.

"The infomorph isn't taking your identity," he wrote back. "It is repurposing social media data into an infomorphic esthetic."

I felt a tightness in my chest.

"#woohoo damn, I'm in the mood for a tidy plate of onion grill with crusty bread. #foodie," @Jon_Ronson tweeted.

I was at war with a robot version of myself.

A month passed. @Jon_Ronson was tweeting twenty times a day about its whirlwind of social engagements, its "soirees," and its wide circle of friends. It now had fifty followers. They were getting a disastrously misrepresentative depiction of my views on soirees and friends.

The spambot left me feeling powerless and sullied. My identity had been redefined all wrong by strangers and I had no recourse.

I tweeted Luke Robert Mason. If he was adamant that he wouldn't take down his spambot, perhaps we could at least meet? I could film the encounter and put it on YouTube. He agreed, writing that he'd be glad to explain the philosophy behind the infomorph. I replied that I'd certainly be interested to learn the philosophy behind the spambot.

I rented a room in central London. I sat there, nervously waiting. On the dot of our prearranged meeting, Luke arrived with two other men—the team behind the spambot. All three were academics. They had met at Warwick University. Luke was the youngest of the three, handsome, in his twenties, a "researcher in technology and cyberculture and director of the Virtual Futures Conference," according to his online CV. David Bausola looked like a rakish teacher, the sort of person who might speak at a conference on the literature of Aleister Crowley. He was a "creative technologist" and the CEO of the digital agency Philter Phactory. Dan O'Hara had a shaved head, and eyes that were piercing and annoyed-looking. His jaw was clenched. He was in his late thirties, a lecturer in English and American literature at the University of Cologne. Before that, he'd been a lecturer at Oxford. He'd coedited a book about J. G. Ballard, *Extreme Metaphors*, and another book, *Thomas Pynchon: Schizophrenia & Social Control*. As far as I understood it, David Bausola had done the actual building of the spambot, while the two other men provided "research and consultancy."

I suggested that they sit in a row on the sofa so I could film them all in a single shot. Dan O'Hara gave the others a glance.

"Let's play along," he said to them. They all sat, with Dan in the middle.

"What do you mean by 'play along'?" I asked him.

"It's about psychological control," he said.

"Do you think my having you in a row on the sofa is my way of psychologically controlling you?" I asked.

"Absolutely," said Dan.

"In what way?" I asked.

"I do that with students," said Dan. "I put myself in a separate chair and put the students in a row on the sofa."

"Why would you want to psychologically control some students?" I asked.

Dan looked briefly worried that he'd been caught saying something eerie. "In order to control the learning environment," he said.

"Is this making you feel uncomfortable?" I asked him.

"No, not really," said Dan. "Are you uncomfortable?"

"Yes," I said.

"Why?" Dan asked.

I spelled out my grievances. "Academics," I began, "don't swoop into a person's life uninvited and use him for some kind of academic exercise, and when I ask you to take it down, you're, *'Oh, it's not a spambot, it's an infomorph.'*"

Dan nodded. He leaned forward. "There must be lots of Jon Ronsons out there?" he began. "People with your name? Yes?"

I looked suspiciously at him. "I'm sure there are people with my name," I replied, carefully.

"I've got the same problem," said Dan, with a smile. He gave me an empathetic look. "There's another academic out there with my name."

"You don't have *exactly* the same problem as I do," I said, "because my *exact* problem is that three strangers have stolen my identity and have created a robot version of me and are refusing to take it down even though they come from respectable universities and give TEDx talks."

Dan let out a long-suffering sigh. "You're saying, 'There is only one Jon Ronson,'" he said. "You're proposing yourself as the real McCoy, as it were, and you want to maintain that integrity and authenticity. Yes?"

I stared at him.

"I think *we* feel annoyed with *you*," Dan continued, "because we're not quite persuaded by that. We think there's already a layer of artifice and it's your online personality—the *brand* Jon Ronson—you're trying to protect. Yeah?"

"NO, IT'S JUST ME TWEETING," I yelled.

"The Internet is not the real world," said Dan.

"I write my tweets," I replied. "And I press send. So it's me on Twitter."

We glared at each other.

"That's not academic," I said. "That's not postmodern. That's the fact of it."

"This is bizarre," Dan said. "I find it really strange—the way you're approaching this. You must be one of the very few people who have chosen to come on Twitter and use their own name as their Twitter name. Who does that? And that's why I'm a little suspicious of your motives, Jon. That's why I say I think you're using it as brand management."

I said nothing, but to this day it kills me that it didn't cross my mind to point out to him that Luke Robert Mason's Twitter name is @LukeRobertMason.

Our conversation continued like this for an hour. I told Dan that I have never used the term *brand management* in my life. "Language like that is alien to me," I said. "And that's the same with your spambot. Its language is different to mine."

"Yes," the three men agreed in unison.

"And that's what's annoying me so much," I explained. "It's a misrepresentation of me."

"You'd like it to be *more* like you?" Dan said.

"I'd like it to not exist," I said.

"That's bizarre," said Dan. He let out an incredulous

whistle. "I find something psychologically interesting about that."

"Why?" I said.

"I find that quite aggressive," he said. "You'd like to *kill* these algorithms? You must feel threatened in some way." He gave me a concerned look. "We don't go around generally trying to kill things we find annoying."

"You're a TROLL!" I yelled.

After the interview was over, I staggered out into the London afternoon. I dreaded uploading the footage onto YouTube because I'd been so screechy. I steeled myself for comments mocking my screechiness and I posted it. I left it up for ten minutes. Then, with apprehension, I had a look.

"This is identity theft," read the first comment I saw. "They should respect Jon's personal liberty."

Wow, I thought, cautiously.

"Somebody should make alternate Twitter accounts of all of those ass clowns and constantly post about their strong desire for child porn," read the next comment.

I grinned.

"These people are manipulative assholes," read the third. "Fuck them. Sue them, break them, destroy them. If I could see these people face to face I would say they are fucking pricks."

I was giddy with joy. I was Braveheart, striding through a field, at first alone, and then it becomes clear that hundreds are marching behind me.

"Vile, disturbing idiots playing with someone else's life

and then laughing at the victim's hurt and anger," read the next comment.

I nodded soberly.

"Utter hateful arseholes," read the next. "These fucked up academics deserve to die painfully. The cunt in the middle is a fucking psychopath."

I frowned slightly. *I hope nobody's going to actually hurt them,* I thought.

"Gas the cunts. Especially middle cunt. And especially left-side bald cunt. And especially quiet cunt. Then piss on their corpses," read the next comment.

I won. Within days, the academics took down @Jon_Ronson. They had been shamed into acquiescence. Their public shaming had been like the button that restores factory settings. Something was out of kilter. The community rallied. The balance was redressed. The academics made a very big meal of eradicating their spambot. They wrote a *Guardian* column explaining that their wider aim was to highlight the tyranny of Wall Street algorithms: "It's not just Ronson who has bots manipulating his life. It's all of us." I still didn't understand why pretending I eat wasabi dumplings might draw the public's attention to the scourge of Wall Street algorithms.

"I have been asked to retire you—do you understand what that means," tweeted David Bausola to the spambot. And, "You have a few hours left. I hope you enjoy them."

"Just press the off switch," I e-mailed him. I tapped my fingers on my desk, impatiently. "Jesus."

I was happy to be victorious. It felt wonderful. The wonderful feeling overwhelmed me like a sedative. Strangers all over the world had united to tell me I was right. It was the perfect ending.

Now I thought back on the other recent social media shamings I'd enjoyed and felt proud of. The first great one happened in October 2009. The Boyzone singer Stephen Gately had been found dead while on holiday with his civil partner, Andrew Cowles. The coroner recorded a verdict of natural causes, but the columnist Jan Moir wrote in the *Daily Mail*, "Whatever the cause of death is, it is not, by any yardstick, a natural one . . . it strikes another blow to the happy-ever-after myth of civil partnerships."

On Twitter we knew what it meant to be the underdog. And here was a member of Britain's elite trying to reshame the gay community and choosing the most callous circumstance to do it. We were not going to tolerate a resurgence of old-time bigotry, and as a result of our collective fury, Marks & Spencer and Nestlé demanded their advertising be removed from the *Daily Mail*'s website. These were great times. We hurt the *Mail* with a weapon they didn't understand—a social media shaming.

After that, when the powerful transgressed, we were there. When the *Daily Mail* mocked a food-bank charity for giving a food parcel to their undercover reporter without running an ID check on him, Twitter responded by donating £39,000 to the charity by the end of that same day.

"This is the nice thing about social media," one tweeter wrote about that campaign. "The *Mail*, which relies primarily on lying to people about their neighbors, can't cope with people communicating among themselves, forming their own opinions."

When LA Fitness refused to cancel the gym membership of a couple who had lost their jobs and couldn't afford the fees, we rallied. LA Fitness hurriedly backed down. These giants were being brought down by people who used to be powerless—bloggers, anyone with a social media account. And the weapon that was felling them was a new one: online shaming.

And then one day it hit me. Something of real consequence was happening. We were at the start of a great renaissance of public shaming. After a lull of almost 180 years (public punishments were phased out in 1837 in the United Kingdom and in 1839 in the United States), it was back in a big way. When we deployed shame, we were utilizing an immensely powerful tool. It was coercive, borderless, and increasing in speed and influence. Hierarchies were being leveled out. The silenced were getting a voice. It was like the democratization of justice. And so I made a decision. The next time a great modern shaming unfolded against some significant wrongdoer—the next time citizen justice prevailed in a dramatic and righteous way—I would leap into the middle of it. I'd investigate it close up and chronicle how efficient it was in righting wrongs.

I didn't have to wait long. @Jon_Ronson was put to death on April 2, 2012. Just twelve weeks later, in the middle of the night on July 4, a man lying on his sofa in Fort Greene, Brooklyn, was looking for ideas for his blog when he made a very unexpected discovery.

Two

I'm Glad I'm Not *That*

In the middle of the night on July 4, 2012, Michael C. Moynihan lay on his sofa. His wife, Joanne, was asleep upstairs with their young daughter. They were broke, as they always were. Everybody seemed to make more money in journalism than Michael did. "I can never turn it into money," he'd later tell me. "I don't know how to do it."

These were anxious times. He was thirty-seven and scraping by as a blogger and a freelancer in a walk-up in a not-great part of Fort Greene, Brooklyn.

But he'd just had a job offer. *The Washington Post* had invited him to blog for ten days. Not that the timing was so great: "It was July Fourth. Everyone was on vacation. There were no readers and there wasn't a lot of news." But still, it was a break. And it was stressing Michael out. The stress had just spoiled a vacation in Ireland visiting his wife's family, and now it was stressing him out on his sofa.

He began hunting around for story ideas. On a whim he downloaded the latest number-one *New York Times* non-fiction bestseller from the young, handsome, and internationally renowned pop-psychology author Jonah Lehrer. It was a book about the neurology of creativity and was called *Imagine: How Creativity Works.*

The first chapter, "Bob Dylan's Brain," piqued Michael's interest, as he was a keen Dylanologist. Jonah Lehrer was reconstructing a critical moment in Dylan's creative career—the thought process that led him to write "Like a Rolling Stone."

It was May 1965 and Dylan was bored, weary from a grueling tour, "skinny from insomnia and pills," sick of his music, thinking he had nothing left to say. As Jonah Lehrer writes:

> The only thing he was sure of was that this life couldn't last. Whenever Dylan read about himself in the newspaper he made the same observation: "God, I'm glad I'm not me," he said. "I'm glad I'm not *that.*"

So Dylan told his manager he was quitting the music business. He moved to a tiny cabin in Woodstock, New York. His plan was to perhaps write a novel.

But then, just when Dylan was most determined to stop creating music, he was overcome with a strange feeling.

"It's a hard thing to describe," Dylan would later remember. "It's just this sense that you got something to say."

It was no wonder *Imagine* had become such a bestseller. Who wouldn't want to read that if they're creatively blocked and feeling hopeless they're just like Bob Dylan immediately before he wrote "Like a Rolling Stone"?

Michael Moynihan, I should explain, hadn't downloaded Jonah Lehrer's book because he was blocked and needed inspirational advice about how to write a *Washington Post* blog. Jonah Lehrer had recently been embroiled in a minor scandal and Michael was considering blogging about it. Some columns he had written for *The New Yorker* had, it turned out, been recycled from columns he'd published months earlier in *The Wall Street Journal*. Michael was considering blogging on how "self-plagiarism" was considered less of a crime in Britain than in America and what that said about the two cultures.

But now Michael suddenly stopped reading. He went back a sentence.

"It's a hard thing to describe," Dylan would later remember. "It's just this sense that you got something to say."

Michael narrowed his eyes. *When the fuck did Bob Dylan say that?* he thought.

"What made you suspicious?" I asked Michael. The two of us were eating lunch at the Cookshop restaurant in Manhattan's Chelsea district. Michael was handsome and fidgety. His eyes were pale and darting like a husky's.

"It just didn't *sound* like Dylan," he said. "In that period, in every interview Dylan did, he was a total asshole to the interviewer. This sounded like a Dylan self-help book."

And so, on his sofa, Michael scanned back a few paragraphs.

> Whenever Dylan read about himself in the newspaper, he made the same observation: "God, I'm glad I'm not me," he said. "I'm glad I'm not *that*."

In D. A. Pennebaker's documentary *Dont Look Back* (the missing apostrophe was the director's idea), Dylan reads an article about himself: "Puffing heavily on a cigarette, he smokes 80 a day . . ." Dylan laughs, "God, I'm glad I'm not me."

How did Jonah Lehrer know that Dylan said this whenever *he read about himself in the paper?* Michael thought. Where did "whenever" come from? Plus, "God, I'm glad I'm not me" is verifiable, but "I'm glad I'm not *that*"? When did he say, "I'm glad I'm not *that*"? Where did Jonah Lehrer get "I'm glad I'm not *that*"?

And so Michael Moynihan e-mailed Jonah Lehrer.

> I picked up your book and as an obsessive Dylan nerd eagerly read the first chapter . . . I'm pretty familiar with

the Dylan canon and there were a few quotes I was
slightly confused by and couldn't locate.

This was Michael's first e-mail to Jonah Lehrer. He was
reading it to me back home in his Fort Greene living room.
Joanne sat with us. There were toys scattered around.

By the time Michael e-mailed Jonah on July 7, he'd pin-
pointed six suspicious Dylan quotes, including "It's just this
sense that you got something to say," "I'm glad I'm not *that*,"
and this angry retort to prying journalists: "I've got nothing
to say about these things I write. I just write them. There's no
great message. Stop asking me to explain."

Dylan did once verifiably say in *Dont Look Back*, "I've got
nothing to say about these things I write. I just write them.
There's no great message."

But there was no "Stop asking me to explain."

Michael mentioned to Jonah his deadline—he was blogging for *The Washington Post* for ten days—and then he
pressed send.

Jonah e-mailed Michael back twice the next day. His e-mails
sounded friendly, professional, businesslike, maybe a little su-
perior. His air was that of a smart young academic understanding Michael's questions and promising to answer them
during an appropriate moment in his schedule. Which would
be in eleven days. He was on vacation in Northern California for ten days. His files were at his home, a seven-hour
drive away. He didn't want to disrupt his vacation by driv-

ing fourteen hours to check his files. If Michael could wait ten days, Jonah would send him detailed notes.

Michael smiled when he read out that part of Jonah's e-mail to me. Eleven days was quite the convenient vacation length given the duration of Michael's *Washington Post* contract.

Still, Jonah said he'd try to answer Michael's questions off the top of his head.

"And this," Michael said, "was where it all began to unravel for him. This is where he makes his first underplayed lie. He's hesitating. 'Do I make this lie?'"

Jonah made the lie.

"I got a little bit of help," he wrote, "from one of Dylan's managers."

This manager had given Jonah access to previously unreleased original transcripts of Dylan interviews. If there were any discrepancies with common references on the Web, that was why.

Jonah's e-mails continued in this vein for several paragraphs: Dylan had told a radio interviewer to "stop asking me to explain" in 1995. The interview was transcribed within the pages of a rare multivolume anthology called *The Fiddler Now Upspoke: A Collection of Bob Dylan's Interviews, Press Conferences and the Like from Throughout the Master's Career*. And so on. Then Jonah thanked Michael for his interest, signed off, and at the bottom of the e-mails were the words "Sent from my iPhone."

"Sent from his iPhone," Michael said. "A rather lengthy e-mail to send from an iPhone. Slightly panicky. Sweaty thumbs, you know?"

Who knew if Jonah Lehrer really was on vacation? But Michael had to take him at his word. So they had a lull. The lull made publication in the *Washington Post* blog impossible, given the digging Michael would need to do. *The Fiddler Now Upspoke* was a nightmare source: "Eleven volumes, twelve volumes, fifteen volumes. Individual ones cost a hundred fifty, two hundred dollars."

Jonah Lehrer presumably thought Michael hadn't the wherewithal to trace, purchase, and scrutinize an anthology as epic and obscure as *The Fiddler Now Upspoke*. But he underestimated the nature of Michael's tenacity. There was something about Michael that reminded me of the cyborg in *Terminator 2*, the one that was even more dogged than Arnold Schwarzenegger, running faster than the fastest car. As Joanne told me, "Michael is the guarder of social rules." She turned to him. "You're a nice guy as long as everyone else . . ."

"When I go out in the world," Michael said, "if someone throws some garbage on the street, it's the most senseless thing to me. I lose my mind. 'Why are you doing this?' "

"And it's for hours," Joanne said. "We're out on a nice walk and it's a half-an-hour rant . . ."

"I see things collapsing," Michael said.

And so Michael tracked down an electronic version of *The Fiddler Now Upspoke*. Well, it wasn't an actual electronic version, but "a complete archive of all known Dylan interviews called *Every Mind-Polluting Word*," Michael told me, "basically a digital version of *Fiddler* that a fan put together and dumped online." It turned out that Bob Dylan had given only one radio interview in 1995 and at no time during it had he told the interviewer to "stop asking me to explain."

On July 11, Michael was in the park with his wife and daughter. It was hot. His daughter was running in and out of the fountain. Michael's phone rang. The voice said, "This is Jonah Lehrer."

I know Jonah Lehrer's voice now. If you had to describe it in a word, that word would be *measured*.

"We had a really nice talk," Michael said, "about Dylan, about journalism. I told him I wasn't trying to make a name for myself with this. I said I'd been grinding away at this for years and I'm just—you know—I do what I do and I feed my family and everything's *okay*."

The way Michael said the word *okay* made it sound like he meant "barely okay." It was the vocal equivalent of a worried head glancing down at the floor.

"I told him I'm not one of those young *Gawker* guys going, 'Find me a target I can burn in the public square and then people will know who I am.' And Jonah said, 'I really appreciate that.'"

Michael liked Jonah. "I got along with him. It was really nice. It was a really nice conversation." They said their good-byes. A few minutes later, Jonah e-mailed Michael to thank him once again for being so decent and not like one of those *Gawker* guys who delight in humiliation. They didn't make them like Michael anymore.

After that, Michael went quiet so he could dig around on Jonah some more.

These were the good days. Michael felt like Hercule Poirot. Jonah's claim that he'd had a little bit of help from one of Dylan's managers had sounded suspiciously vague, Michael had thought. And, indeed, it turned out that Bob Dylan had only one manager. His name was Jeff Rosen. And although Jeff Rosen's e-mail address was hard to come by, Michael came by it.

Michael e-mailed him. Had Jeff Rosen ever spoken to Jonah Lehrer? Jeff Rosen replied that he never had.

So Michael e-mailed Jonah to say he had some more questions.

Jonah replied, sounding surprised. Was Michael still going to write something? He assumed Michael wasn't going to write anything.

Michael shook his head with incredulity when he recounted this part to me. Jonah had obviously convinced himself that he'd sweet-talked Michael out of investigating him. But no. "Bad liars always think they're good at it," Michael said to me. "They're always confident they're defeating you."

"I've spoken to Jeff Rosen," Michael told Jonah.

And that, Michael said, is when Jonah lost it. "He just lost it. I've never seen anyone like it."

• • •

Jonah started repeatedly telephoning Michael, pleading with him not to publish. Sometimes Michael would silence his iPhone for a while. Then he'd return to find so many missed calls from Jonah that he would take a screenshot because nobody would otherwise have believed it. I asked Michael at what point it stopped being fun, and he replied, "When your quarry starts panicking." He paused. "It's like being out in the woods hunting and you're, 'This feels great!' And then you shoot the animal and it's lying there twitching and wants its head to be bashed in and you're, 'I don't want to be the person to do this. This is fucking *horrible.*'"

Michael got a call from Jonah's agent, Andrew Wylie. He represents not just Jonah but also Bob Dylan and Salman Rushdie and David Bowie and David Byrne and David Rockefeller and V. S. Naipaul and *Vanity Fair* and Martin Amis and Bill Gates and King Abdullah II of Jordan and Al Gore. Actually, Andrew Wylie didn't phone Michael. "He got in touch with somebody who got in touch with me to tell me to call him," Michael told me. "Which I thought was very *Tinker Tailor Soldier Spy.* He's thought to be the most powerful literary agent in the United States and I'm a schlub, I'm a nobody. So I called him. I laid out the case. He said, 'If you publish this, you're going to ruin a guy's life. Do you think this is a big enough deal to ruin a guy's life?'"

"How did you reply?" I asked.

"I said, 'I'll think about it,'" Michael said. "I guess Andrew Wylie is a bazillionaire because he's very perceptive, because I got a call from Jonah, who said, 'So Andrew Wylie says you're going to go ahead and publish.'"

On the afternoon of Sunday, July 29, Michael was walking down Flatbush Avenue, on the telephone to Jonah, shouting at him, "'I need you to go on the record. You have to do it, Jonah. You have to go on the record.' My arms were going crazy. I was so angry and so frustrated. All the time he was wasting. All his lies. And he was simpering." Finally something in Jonah's voice made Michael know that it was going to happen. "So I ran into Duane Reade, and I bought a fucking Hello Kitty notebook and a pen, and in twenty-five seconds, he said, 'I panicked. And I'm deeply sorry for lying.'"

"And there you go," said Michael. "It's done."

Twenty-six days, and it took Michael forty minutes to write the story. He'd still not worked out how to make money from journalism. He'd agreed to give the scoop to a small Jewish online magazine, *Tablet*. Knowing how lucky they were, the people at *Tablet* paid Michael quadruple what they usually pay, but it was quadruple of not much: $2,200 total—which is all he'd ever make from the story.

Forty minutes to write it, and what felt to him like nine packs of cigarettes.

"If anything, Jonah Lehrer nearly killed *me* I smoked so many fucking cigarettes out on the fire escape. Smoking, smoking, smoking. When you have the ability to press send on something and really, really affect the outcome of the rest of that person's life. And the phone was ringing and ringing and ringing and ringing. There were twenty-odd missed calls from Jonah that Sunday night. Twenty-four missed calls, twenty-five missed calls."

"He kept phoning," Joanne said. "It was so sad. I don't understand why he thought it was a good idea to keep phoning."

"It was the worst night of his life," I said.

"Yeah, yeah, for sure, for sure," Michael said.

Finally, Michael picked up the phone. "I said, 'Jonah, you have to stop calling me. This is almost to the point of harassment.' I felt like I was talking him off the ledge. I said, 'Tell me you're not going to do anything stupid.' It was that level of panic. So much so that I thought maybe I should pull back from this. He was, *'Please, please, please,'* like a child's toy breaking, droning, running out of batteries, *'Please please, please . . .'*"

Michael asked me if I'd ever been in that position. Had I ever stumbled on a piece of information that, if published, would destroy someone? Actually *destroy* them.

I thought for a while. "Destroy someone?" I said. I paused. "No. I don't think so. I'm not sure."

"Don't ever do it," he said.

Michael said he honestly considered not pressing send that night. Jonah had a young daughter the same age as Michael's young daughter. Michael said he couldn't kid himself. He understood what pressing send would mean to Jonah's life: "What we do, when we fuck up, we don't lose our job. We lose our *vocation*."

Michael was thinking of former journalists like *The New Republic*'s Stephen Glass. Glass was the author of a celebrated 1998 story, "Hack Heaven," about a fifteen-year-old schoolboy hacker who was offered a job with a software company he'd hacked into. Glass wrote about being a fly-on-the-wall in the company's offices—Jukt Micronics—as the boy negotiated his terms:

> "I want more money. I want a Miata. I want a trip to Disney World. I want X-Men comic number one. I want a lifetime subscription to *Playboy*—and throw in *Penthouse*. Show me the money! Show me the money!" Across the table, executives . . . are listening and trying ever so delicately to oblige. "Excuse me, sir," one of the suits says tentatively to the pimply teenager. "Excuse me. Pardon me for interrupting you, sir. We can arrange more money for you."
>
> —STEPHEN GLASS, "WASHINGTON SCENE:
> HACK HEAVEN," *The New Republic*, MAY 18, 1998

But there was no conference room, no Jukt Micronics, no schoolboy hacker. A *Forbes* digital journalist, Adam Penenberg, annoyed that *The New Republic* had scooped him on his own turf, did some digging and discovered that Glass had invented it all. Glass was fired. He later enrolled in law school, earned a degree magna cum laude, applied in 2014 to practice law in California, and was refused. Glass's shaming was following him around wherever he went, like Pigpen's cloud of dirt. In some ways, he and Jonah Lehrer were eerily alike—young, nerdy, Jewish, preternaturally successful journalists on a roll who made things up. But Glass had invented entire scenarios, casts of characters, reams of dialogue. Jonah's "I'm glad I'm not *that*" at the end of "I'm glad I'm not me" was stupid and wrong, but a world that doled out punishments as merciless as that would be unfathomable to me. I thought Michael was being overly dramatic to believe that pressing send would sentence Jonah to Stephen Glass–level oblivion.

In the end, it was all academic for Michael. He said he felt as trapped in this story as Jonah was. It was like they were both in a car with failed brakes, hurtling helplessly toward this ending together. How could Michael not press send? What would people think if the story got out? That he'd covered it up for career advancement? "I would have been the spineless so-called journalist who buckled to Andrew Wylie. I never would have worked again."

Plus, Michael said, something had happened a few hours earlier that he felt made it impossible for him to bury the story. After Jonah had confessed over the phone to him, Michael was shaking, so he went to a café in Park Slope, Brooklyn, to calm down. It was the Café Regular du Nord. As he sat outside, he ran into a fellow writer, *Vanity Fair*'s Dana Vachon.

"I'm doing this story and this guy just fucking confessed to me that it's all *phony*," Michael told him.

"Who?" Dana Vachon replied.

"I can't tell you," Michael said.

That second Michael's phone rang. The screen flashed up the words JONAH LEHRER.

"Oh," Dana Vachon said. "Jonah Lehrer."

"Fuck you!" Michael said. "You can't say anything!"

So now Dana Vachon knew. Michael's editors at *Tablet* knew. Andrew Wylie knew. It was not going to stay contained. So Michael pressed send.

Michael had one final telephone conversation with Jonah after they both knew it was over. It was just a few hours before the story appeared. Michael had barely slept that night. He was exhausted. He said to Jonah, "I just want you to know that it makes me feel like shit to do this."

"And Jonah paused," Michael told me. "And then he said to me, no joke, he said, 'You know, I really don't care how you feel.'" Michael shook his head. "It was icy."

Then Jonah said to Michael, "I really, really regret . . ."

Regret what? Michael thought. *Cheating? Lying?*

"I really regret ever responding to your e-mail," Jonah said.

"And my response to him," Michael said, "was basically silence."

That night Michael was "shattered. I felt horrible. I'm not a fucking monster. I was crushed and depressed. My wife can confirm this." He replayed in his mind his telephone conversations with Jonah. Suddenly, he felt suspicious. Maybe the icy Jonah from that final conversation had been the real Jonah all along. Maybe Jonah had been playing Michael all that time, "cranking the emotions" to guilt-trip him. Maybe Jonah had assessed Michael as "pliable and easy to manipulate." When Michael had told Jonah that he'd spoken to Jeff Rosen, Jonah's reply had been "Then I guess you're a better journalist than me." That suddenly sounded incredibly condescending to Michael, like he saw Michael as just "some putz piddling around trying to pick up freelance work." Maybe everything Jonah had done during the previous weeks was, in fact, devious and very well plotted.

I wondered: *Had Jonah really been devious, or just terrified? Was Michael conjuring up words like* devious *in an attempt to feel less bad?* Devious is creepy. Terrified is human.

"Having a phone conversation with somebody is like reading a novel," Michael said. "Your mind creates a scenario. I sort of knew what he looked like from his author jacket photos, but I'd never seen him move. I didn't know his gait. I didn't know his clothes. Well, I knew he posed in his hipster glasses. But over those four weeks, I was imagining this character. I was picturing his house. A little house. He's a journalist. I'm a journalist. I'm a fucking schlub. I pay my rent. I'm fine, I'm happy, but I'm not doing great."

This was about the third time Michael had described himself to me as a "schlub" or something similar. I suppose he knew that highlighting this aspect of himself made for the most dramatic, likable retelling of the collision between the two men. The nobody blogger and the crooked VIP. David and Goliath. But I wondered if he was doing it for more than just storytelling reasons. All the stuff he said about how it wasn't his fault that he stumbled onto the story, how he made no money from it, how the stress nearly killed him, how he was actually trapped into it by Andrew Wylie and Dana Vachon . . . it suddenly hit me: Michael was traumatized by what he had done. When he'd said to me, "Don't ever do it"—don't ever press send on a story that would destroy someone—it wasn't a figure of speech. He meant it.

"I was picturing his house, a little house," Michael continued. "I was transferring my life onto his. His wife's bustling around, his kid's in the background, he's in one of the two bedrooms at the back, sweating." Michael paused. "And then my friend from the *Los Angeles Times* sent me a story from 2009 about the purchase of the Julius Shulman house."

The Hollywood Hills residence and studio of the late iconic photographer Julius Shulman has sold for $2.25 million. The Midcentury Modern steel-frame house, built in 1950 and designed by Raphael S. Soriano, is a Los Angeles historic landmark. The buyer is bestselling author and lecturer Jonah Lehrer. His book "How We Decide" has been translated into a dozen languages. The writer has an affinity for classic design.

—Lauren Beale, *Los Angeles Times*, December 4, 2010

The Shulman House. Photograph by Michael K. Wilkinson,
reproduced with his permission.

"It's unfair," Michael said. "It's stupid of me. In some ways it's unconscionable to begrudge him his success. But it made things a bit different."

• • •

A few weeks after Michael told me his Jonah Lehrer story, I was at a party in London, talking to a man I didn't know. He was a theater director. He asked me what I was writing about and I told him about Michael and Jonah. Sometimes, when I recount for people the stories I'm working on, I feel a stupid grin on my face as I describe the absurdity of whatever crazy pickle this or that interviewee had got himself into. But not this time. As I related the details to him, the director shivered. And I found myself shivering too. When I finished the story, he said, "It's about the terror, isn't it?"

"The terror of what?" I said.

"The terror of being found out," he said.

He looked as if he felt he were taking a risk even mentioning to me the existence of the terror. He meant that we all have ticking away within us something we fear will badly harm our reputation if it got out—some "I'm glad I'm not *that*" at the end of an "I'm glad I'm not me." I think he was right. Maybe our secret is actually nothing horrendous. Maybe nobody would even consider it a big deal if it was exposed. But we can't take that risk. So we keep it buried. Maybe it's a work impropriety. Or maybe it's just a feeling that at any moment we'll blurt something out during some important meeting that'll prove to everyone that we aren't proper professional people or, in fact, functional human beings. I think that even in these days of significant oversharing we keep this particular terror concealed, like people used to with things like masturbation before everyone suddenly got blasé about it online. With masturbation, nobody cares. Whereas our reputation—it's everything.

I had leaped into the middle of the Michael–Jonah story because I admired Michael and identified with him. He personified citizen justice, whereas Jonah represented literary fraud in the pop-science world. He made a fortune corrupting an already self-indulgent, bloated genre. I still admired Michael. But suddenly, when the theater director said the words *the terror of being found out*, I felt like a door had briefly opened before me, revealing some infinite horror land filled with millions of scared-stiff Jonahs. How many people had I banished to that land during my thirty years of journalism? How truly nightmarish it must have been to be Jonah Lehrer.

Three

The Wilderness

Runyon Canyon, West Hollywood. If you were a passing hiker and you didn't know that Jonah Lehrer had been totally destroyed, you wouldn't have guessed it. He looked like he did in his old author photographs—pleasing to the eye, a little aloof, as if he were thinking higher thoughts and expressing them in a considered manner to his fellow hiker—me. But we weren't having a considered conversation. For the last hour, Jonah had been repeatedly telling me, in a voice strained to its breaking point, "I don't belong in your book."

And I was repeatedly replying, "Yes, you do."

I didn't understand what he was talking about. I was writing a book about public shaming. He had been publicly shamed. He was ideal.

Now he suddenly stopped in the middle of the hiking trail

and looked intently at me. "I am a terrible story to put in your book," he said.

"Why?" I said.

"What's that William Dean Howells line?" he said. "'Americans like a tragedy with a happy ending'?"

The actual William Dean Howells line is "What the American public wants in the theater is a tragedy with a happy ending." I think Jonah was close enough.

I was here because Jonah's shaming felt to me like a really important one—the shape of things to come. He was a dishonest, number-one bestselling author who had been exposed by the sort of person who used to be powerless. And despite seeing Jonah's face etched in panic and misery on the hiking trail, I was sure the renaissance in public shaming was a good thing. Look at who was being laid low—bigoted *Daily Mail* columnists, monolithic gym chains with pitiless cancellation policies, and, most heinous of all, horrific academic spambot creators. Jonah had written some very good things during his short career. Some of his work had been wonderful. But he had repeatedly transgressed, he had done bad things, and the uncovering of his lies was appropriate.

Still, as we walked, I felt for Jonah. Close-up, I could see he was suffering terribly. Michael had called his cover-up a "great deception that was very, very well plotted." But I think it was just chaos, and on that last day before the story broke, Jonah wasn't "icy" but wrecked.

"I'm just drenched in shame and regret," he had e-mailed me before I flew to Los Angeles to meet him. "The shaming process is fucking brutal."

Jonah was offering the same dismal prediction about his

future as Michael and Andrew Wylie had offered. He was foreseeing a lifetime of ruin. Imagine being thirty-one in a country that venerates redemption and second chances, and convinced your tragedy has no happy ending. But I thought he was being too pessimistic. Surely, after paying some penance, after spending some time in the wilderness, he could convince his readers and peers that he could change his ways. He could find a way back in. I mean, we weren't monsters.

. . .

Science writing had been Jonah Lehrer's ambition from the start. After he'd agreed to meet me, I found an old interview he gave ten years ago, when he was twenty-one.

> [He] hopes to become a science writer. "Science is too often perceived as cold," he says. "I want to translate science and show how beautiful it can be."
>
> —KRISTIN STERLING, *Columbia News*, DECEMBER 2002

That interview was published on the occasion of the announcement that Jonah had been awarded a Rhodes Scholarship to study at Oxford as a graduate student for two years. "Each year 32 young Americans are selected as Rhodes Scholars," according to the Rhodes Scholarship website, "chosen not only for their outstanding scholarly achievements, but for their character, commitment to others and to the common good."

Bill Clinton had been a Rhodes Scholar, as had the cosmologist Edwin Hubble, and the film director Terrence Malick. In 2002 only two Columbia students were awarded the accolade—Jonah Lehrer and Cyrus Habib, who is now, ten years on, one of the few fully blind American politicians and the highest-ranking Iranian-American in political office in the United States, serving in the Washington state legislature. Cyrus Habib sounds amazing.

Jonah began writing his first book, *Proust Was a Neuroscientist*, while he was still a Rhodes Scholar at Oxford. Its premise is that the great neuroscience breakthroughs of today had all been made one hundred years ago by artists like Cézanne and Proust. It was a lovely book. Jonah was smart and he wrote well—which isn't the same as saying Mussolini made the trains run on time. Jonah wrote good things throughout his short career, essays untainted by transgression. After *Proust* came *How We Decide* and, last, *Imagine*. Along the way, Jonah earned a fortune giving inspirational keynotes at—to name a few of the innumerable conferences he spoke at that I had never heard of—the 2011 International Association of Business Communicators World Conference in San Diego; FUSION, the Eighth Annual Desire2Learn Users Conference in Denver; and the 2012 Grantmakers for Effective Organizations National Conference in Seattle.

At this last one he told the story of a young athlete—a high jumper who could never clear the bar, however hard he tried. All the other jumpers mocked him. But then he thought counterintuitively about it, invented a new jumping style that would be called the Fosbury Flop, and won the 1968 Olympic gold medal. By now, Jonah was commanding vast speaker fees—tens of thousands of dollars. I suppose he was being rewarded so richly because his messages were inspirational. My talks tend to be more disincentivizing, which, I have noticed, pays less.

The adjective most often applied to Jonah was "Gladwellian," Malcolm Gladwell being the *New Yorker* writer and author of the era's most successful counterintuitive pop-science book, *The Tipping Point*. Jonah's book jackets looked like Malcolm Gladwell's book jackets. Their jackets looked like Apple computer packaging. Jonah was becoming a sensation. When he switched jobs, it was a news story.

JONAH LEHRER JUMPS FROM WIRED
TO THE NEW YORKER

Jonah Lehrer, the author of the popular science books "Proust Was a Scientist [*sic*]," "How We Decide" and 2012's "Imagine," has left his post as a contributing editor at Wired for the New Yorker, where he'll be a staff writer.

In many ways, Lehrer is a younger, brain-centered version of Gladwell, making him a natural New Yorker fit.

—CAROLYN KELLOGG, *Los Angeles Times*, JUNE 7, 2012

Jonah resigned from *The New Yorker* after seven weeks in the job, the day Michael's article appeared. On the Sunday night before publication, Jonah had been giving a keynote at the 2012 Meeting Professionals International's World Education Congress in St. Louis. The subject of his talk was the importance of human interaction. During the talk—

according to a tweet posted by an audience member, the journalist Sarah Braley—Jonah revealed that since the invention of Skype, attendance at meetings had actually gone *up* by 30 percent. After he left the stage, Sarah found him and asked where that implausible statistic had come from. "A conversation with a Harvard professor," he replied. But when she requested the professor's name, he mysteriously refused to divulge it. "I'd have to ask him if it's all right to tell you," he explained. She gave Jonah her card but never heard from him, which didn't surprise her because the next morning he was disgraced and resigned his job.

In the days that followed, Jonah's publisher withdrew and pulped every copy of *Imagine* still in circulation, and offered refunds to all who had bought one. The Dylan quotes had been enough to bring Jonah down. His subsequent panic spiral was *definitely* enough—Michael wrote in his exposé that Jonah had "stonewalled, misled, and, eventually, outright lied" to him. Internet message boards were replete with comments like "The twerp is such a huge over-achiever that there's something delightful about seeing him humbled" (*The Guardian*) and "Save the royalties from your book, blockhead, 'cause you're gonna need the money" (*The New York Times*) and "It must be strange to be so full of lies" (*Tablet*).

In Brooklyn, Michael was agonizing over whether he'd been right to press send. Although he'd essentially seen his takedown of Jonah as a righteous strike against the pop-science genre—"To make a tight little package where my mother would be like, 'Ooh, I just read this thing, did you know that X leads to Y,' you have to fucking cut corners"—

Andrew Wylie's words were haunting him. Maybe it wasn't enough to ruin a man's life over.

But there was worse to come. *Wired* magazine asked the journalism professor Charles Seife to study eighteen columns Jonah had written for them. All but one, he reported, revealed "evidence of some journalistic misdeed." It was mainly Jonah reusing his own sentences in different stories, but that wasn't all. Imagine if I had failed to put quotation marks around the sentences I lifted earlier from the Rhodes Scholarship website. It was that kind of pervasive sloppiness/plagiarism. Probably the worst infraction was that Jonah had taken some paragraphs from a blog written by Christian Jarrett of the British Psychological Society and passed them off as his own.

Michael was massively relieved—he told me—that "the rot spidered out to every book, every piece of journalism."

Jonah vanished, leaving a final, innocent prehumiliation tweet like a plate of congealing food on the *Mary Celeste*.

Fiona Apple's new album is "astonishing," rhapsodizes @sfj.

—@JONAHLEHRER, JUNE 18, 2012

He ignored all interview requests. He resurfaced only once, to briefly tell *Los Angeles* magazine's Amy Wallace that he wasn't giving any interviews. So it was a great surprise when he responded to my e-mail. He was "happy to be in touch," he wrote me, and "happy to chat on the phone or whatever." In the end, we arranged to go hiking in the Hollywood Hills. I flew to Los Angeles even though his final e-mail to me included an unexpected and unsettling sentence toward the end: "I'm not sure I'm ready to be a case study or talk on the record."

It seemed appropriate that we were hiking in a desert canyon, because his punishment felt quite biblical, a public shaming followed by a casting out into the wilderness, although that analogy only went so far because biblical wildernesses tend not to be filled with extremely beautiful movie stars and models walking their dogs.

We walked in silence for a while. Then Jonah listed two more reasons (alongside the "Americans want tragedies with happy endings" one) why I shouldn't write about him. First, if I was planning to be kind to him, he didn't deserve it. And, second, a warning: "What I mostly feel is intensely radioactive. So even people who come to me with good intentions, I end up transferring my isotopes onto them."

Jonah was saying that spending time with him would ruin *me* in some unexpected way. "Well, that's not going to happen to me!" I laughed.

"Then you'll be the first," he said.

As he said this, a bolt of panic shot into me. It was a frightening thing for someone to say. Still, I kept trying to convince him, on and on, but each line of reasoning seemed to make him more anguished, as if I were a siren trying to lure him to the rocks with my song of possible redemption. He said his worst days were when he allowed himself to hope for a second chance. The best were when he knew it was over forever and his destruction was necessary as a deterrent to others.

I gave up. Jonah drove me back to my hotel. In the car I stared at my lap, exhausted, like a cold-caller after a long shift. Then, suddenly, Jonah said, "I've decided to make a public apology."

I looked up at him. "Have you?"

"Next week," Jonah said. "In Miami. At a Knight lunch."

The John S. and James L. Knight Foundation was created by the owners of the *Chicago Daily News* and *The Miami Herald* to fund young journalists with innovative ideas. There was to be a conference for the fund organizers, Jonah said, and he'd been asked to deliver the after-lunch keynote on the final day. As an advocate of digital media, the foundation planned to broadcast his speech live on its website.

"I keep writing and scrapping and rewriting it," Jonah said. "Would you read it over? Maybe after that we can discuss whether I fit your narrative?"

• • •

I am the author of a book on creativity that is best known because it contained several fabricated Bob Dylan quotes. I committed plagiarism on my blog. I lied, repeatedly, to a journalist named Michael Moynihan to cover up the Dylan fabrications.

I sat on the plane reading Jonah's apology speech. It was a stark opening—an unembellished declaration of guilt, followed by an account of his shame and regret.

I think about all the readers I've disappointed, people who paid good money for my book and now don't want it on their shelves.

I was surprised by his candor. Jonah had insisted on our hike that if he did decide to give me an interview the one off-limit topic would be the shame. It was too private and personal, he said. But by the next sentence, it became clear that the shame was something he intended to deal with as hurriedly as possible on the way to something else. This was, it quickly became clear, an apology speech like no other. He was going to explain his flaws within the context of neuroscience. It was a Jonah Lehrer keynote speech on the unique flaws of smart people like Jonah Lehrer. He began comparing himself to inadvertently imperfect scientists working at the FBI forensics lab. Innocent people had been convicted of terrorism because brilliant FBI scientists were "victims of their hidden brain, undone by flaws so deep-seated they don't even notice their existence."

He gave an example—an Oregon lawyer, Brandon Mayfield, who was falsely accused by the FBI of committing the Madrid bombings of March 2004. A fingerprint had been lifted from a bag of detonators found at the scene. After the FBI fed it into their database, Mayfield's name came back as a match.

The detectives soon discovered that Mayfield was a Muslim, married to an Egyptian immigrant, and had represented a convicted terrorist in a child custody dispute.

The FBI held Mayfield for two weeks before acknowledging that the fingerprint match was "not even close." In fact, the agency had fallen victim to something known as confirmation bias. It was taking seriously only those pieces of information that confirmed the preexisting belief that Mayfield was the culprit. It was unconsciously filtering out evidence that pointed to his innocence. As a result of the scandal, the FBI implemented rigorous new reforms to root out errors. It would be great—Jonah ended his speech by saying—if something like that could happen with him.

If I'm lucky enough to write again, I won't write a thing that isn't fact-checked and fully footnoted. Because here is what I've learned: unless I'm willing to continually grapple with my failings—until I'm forced to fix my first draft, and deal with criticism of the second, and submit the final for a good, independent scrubbing—I won't create anything worth keeping around.

This was the happy ending Jonah believed Americans wanted. As I sat on the plane, I realized I had no idea if his speech was good or bad, or if it would go down poorly or well. The FBI stuff was overly tangential and evasive. Jonah wasn't really like the FBI. As it happens, I've done my own research on the perils of confirmation bias and agree with Jonah that it is a powerful bias indeed, often found at the heart of miscarriages of justice. In fact, ever since I first learned about confirmation bias, I've been seeing it everywhere. Everywhere. But even a confirmation bias aficionado like me could see that Jonah hadn't succumbed to it. Deliberately padding out Bob Dylan quotes to fit a thesis about the creative process wasn't confirmation bias.

So I found the FBI digression a bit slippery, but there was still a good chance his speech could be like the end of Neil Diamond's *The Jazz Singer,* where the disgraced synagogue cantor wins over the congregation by reminding them how beautiful his singing voice is. I e-mailed Jonah to say I thought his speech was fantastic. He sent me an appreciative reply. I asked him if I could come with him to Miami. He said no.

•   •   •

I am the author of a book on creativity that . . . contained several fabricated Bob Dylan quotes . . . I lied to a journalist named Michael Moynihan.

Jonah was at the Knight Foundation lectern, standing very still. I was watching at home on my computer. In his old lucrative public-speaking days, his voice would rise and fall to emphasize this word or that, but now he sounded flat, like a scared child in front of the class. This was the most important speech of his life. He was begging for a second chance. If things weren't stressful enough for him, the Knight Foundation had decided to erect a giant screen behind his head that displayed a live Twitter feed. Anyone watching from home could tweet their ongoing opinion of Jonah's request for forgiveness using the hashtag #infoneeds and their comment would automatically appear, in real time and in gigantic letters, right next to Jonah's face. A second screen was positioned within his sightline.

I saw Jonah's eyes flicker to it.

> Wow. Jonah Lehrer talk dives directly into a listing of failures, errors and mea culpa.

> And that, people, is how you apologize.

During the preceding seven months, Jonah had been disgraced and ridiculed and cast out. He had shuffled along the canyons of Los Angeles in a never-ending sweat of guilt and shame, a constant clenched pain. And now, suddenly, there was light. I felt as if I were witnessing a kind of miracle. Just like with my spambot men, we knew when to shame and when to stop. It was as if we instinctively understood that Jonah's punishment had reached an appropriate peak and now it was time to listen to what he had to say.

And then Jonah moved on to the FBI analogy.

* * *

I'd like to tell you a story that has given me a little hope. It's a story about a mistake and how it was fixed. It's a story that I was working on at the time my career fell apart. The story is about forensic science.

It quickly became extremely clear to Jonah, and to me watching at home, that the audience had no interest in his opinions on forensic science. Perhaps they would have had at some point in his career. But not anymore.

> Jonah Lehrer boring people into forgiving
> him for his plagiarism.

> I am not feeling terribly convinced
> by the deadpan mea culpa droning on
> by @JonahLehrer.

> I can't handle watching the @JonahLehrer
> apology. He is boring and unconvincing.
> Time for something else.

Jonah carried on. He talked of how, a month before he resigned from his job, he interviewed the behavioral economist Dan Ariely on the subject of how "the human mind is a confabulation machine."

> "The human mind is a confabulation machine."
> Now *that's* passing the buck.

> Using shoddy Pop-psych to explain inability to
> even write shoddy Pop-psych from scratch.

> Jonah Lehrer is a friggin' sociopath.

Trapped at the lectern, Jonah had twenty minutes of his speech to go, followed by the Q&A.

I agreed with the tweeter who wrote that Jonah was pass-

ing the buck when he said that the human mind was "a confabulation machine." But by mid-apology, it seemed irrelevant
whether the criticisms had legitimacy. They were cascading
into his sightline in a torrent. Jonah was being told in the
most visceral, instantaneous way that there was no forgiveness for him, no possibility of reentry.

> The only way @JonahLehrer can redeem
> himself from his failures is by doing completely
> different work. He is tainted as a writer forever.

> I have zero inclination to forgive or read his
> future work.

> Rantings of a Delusional, Unrepentant
> Narcissist.

> Jonah Lehrer's speech should be titled
> "Recognizing self-deluded assholes and
> how to avoid them in the future."

Still, he was forced to continue. He had no choice. He had
to reach the end. He flatly intoned that he hoped that one day,
"when I tell my young daughter the same story I've just told
you, I will be a better person because of it. More humble."

> Wait, Jonah Lehrer is speaking at a journalism
> conference? Did they run out of people who
> aren't frauds with interesting stuff to say?

> Jonah Lehrer putting on a great demonstration
> of the emptiness of pop behavior-psych: a
> moral defective tries to blame cognitive failure.

> He has not proven that he is capable of feeling
> shame.

The speech ended with a polite round of applause from the people in the same room as he was.

Amid the tidal wave of abuse, there had been some calls for humanity, a few tweeters noting the terrible strangeness of what was unfolding.

> Ugh, Jonah Lehrer is apologizing next to a
> live Twitter feed of people mocking him. It's
> basically a 21st century town square flogging.

> Jonah Lehrer is a real person. Twitter is making
> me so uncomfortable right now.

> Jonah Lehrer's crimes are significant, but
> apologizing in front of a giant-screen Twitter
> feed seems cruel and unusual punishment.

But all that was wiped away when someone tweeted: *Did Lehrer get paid to be there today?*
Of course he didn't, I thought.
And then Knight answered that question.

> Jonah Lehrer was paid $20K to speak about
> plagiarism at Knight lunch.

Wish I could get paid $20,000 to say that I'm a
lying dirtbag.

And so on, until late that evening, when this tweet arrived.

Journalism foundation apologizes for paying
$20,000 to disgraced author Jonah Lehrer.

Jonah e-mailed. "Today was really awful. I'm filled with
all sorts of regret."

I sent him a sympathetic reply. I said I thought he should
donate the $20,000 to charity.

"Nothing can turn this around," he replied. "I've got to be
realistic about that. I shouldn't have accepted the invitation
to speak, but now it's too late."

• • •

F uck off, you can't even do your apology without slotting it
into some stupid Jonah framework," Michael Moynihan
said to me over lunch at Cookshop in New York City. Michael
shook his head in wonder. "That wasn't an apology. It was a
string of Gladwellian bullshit. He was on autopilot. He was
a robot: 'Let me get this study from some academic.' All the
words he used to describe his dishonesty. It was like a thesau-
rus had landed on his head." Michael paused. "Oh!" he said.
"Someone sent me a text. I thought he was reading way too
much into it. But he pointed out to me that Jonah said, 'I lied
to a journalist CALLED Michael Moynihan.' I love that. I
said, 'Yeah. I see what you're saying.' He didn't lie to 'journal-

ist Michael Moynihan.' That's the great trick of the language. 'A journalist CALLED Michael Moynihan.' 'Who's this fucking schlub?'"

Michael took a bite of his steak. The fact was, his was a great scoop. It was great journalism, and what did Michael get from it? Some congratulatory tweets, which probably give you a bit of a dopamine rush or something, but otherwise nothing: $2,200 plus a veiled insult from Jonah if Michael and his friend weren't being paranoid about that part.

Michael shook his head. "Nothing came out of this for me," he said.

In fact, it was worse than nothing. Michael had noticed that people were starting to feel scared of him. Fellow journalists. A few days before our lunch, some panicked writer—someone Michael barely knew—had confessed out of the blue that a biography he'd written might have inadvertently veered into plagiarism.

"Like I *adjudicate* these things," said Michael.

Whether Michael liked it or not, there was fear in the air now because of what had happened to Jonah. But Michael didn't want to be some witchfinder general, roaming the countryside with writers blurting out declarations of guilt to him, begging his forgiveness for crimes he hadn't known they'd committed.

"You turn around and you suddenly realize you're the head of a pitchfork mob," Michael said. "And it's 'What are these people fucking *doing* here? Why are they acting like heathens? I don't want to be associated with this at all. I want to get out of here.'"

"It was *horrible*," I said. "All this time I'd been thinking we were in the middle of some kind of idealistic reimagining of the justice system. But those people were so *cold*."

The response to Jonah's apology had been brutal and confusing to me. It felt as if the people on Twitter had been invited to be characters in a courtroom drama, and had been allowed to choose their roles, and had all gone for the part of the hanging judge. Or it was even worse than that. They all had gone for the part of the people in the lithographs being ribald at whippings.

"I'm watching people stabbing and stabbing and stabbing Jonah," Michael said, "and I'm, 'HE'S *DEAD*.'"

• • •

The next day I drove from New York to Boston to visit the Massachusetts Archives and the Massachusetts Historical Society. Given how vicious the resurgence of public shaming had suddenly turned, I wondered why that type of punishment had been phased out in the nineteenth century. I had assumed—like most people do, I think—that this demise was due to the migration from villages to cities. Shame became ineffectual because pilloried people could lose themselves in the anonymous crowd as soon as the chastisement was over. Shame had lost its power to shame. That was my assumption. Was it right?

I parked my car outside the Massachusetts Archives, a

slablike Brutalist building on the waterfront near the John F. Kennedy Presidential Library and Museum. Inside were the microfilms that preserve early legal documents handwritten by the Puritan settlers. I took my seat at a microfilm reader and began to carefully scroll through them. For the first hundred years, as far as I could tell, all that happened in America was that various people named Nathaniel had purchased land near rivers. The spindly words swirled on the fraying pages. They really should have spent more time on paragraph breaks back then and less time on the letter *f*. I began to speed up, scrolling unprofessionally, decades passing before me in seconds, until I suddenly found myself face-to-face with an early American shaming.

It was July 15, 1742. A woman named Abigail Gilpin, her husband at sea, was found "naked in bed with one John Russell." They were both to be "whipped at the public whipping post twenty stripes each." Abigail was not appealing the whipping itself, but was begging the judge to "let me have my punishment before the people are stirring. If your honor pleases, take some pity on me for my dear children, who cannot help their mother's unfortunate failings."

The documents don't reveal whether the judge consented, but straight after that, I found a transcript of a sermon that offered a clue as to why she might have pled for a private whipping. The sermon, by the Reverend Nathan Strong of Hartford, Connecticut, was an entreaty to people to be less exuberant at executions: "Do not go to that place of horror with elevated spirits, and gay hearts, for death is there! Justice and judgment are there! The power of government, displayed in its most awful form, is there . . . The person who can go and look on death merely to gratify an idle humor is destitute both of humanity and piety."

After lunch, I traveled the few miles to the Massachusetts Historical Society, a grand old townhouse on Boylston Street. I remembered something Jonah had e-mailed me before I flew to Los Angeles: "The shaming process is fucking brutal." I thought about the phrase "shaming process." It was probably reassuring for a shamee to envisage their punishment as a process rather than a free-for-all. If you're being destroyed, you want to feel that the people tearing you apart at least know what they're doing. Well, maybe less delicate shamees wouldn't care how orderly their shaming was, but Jonah struck me as someone for whom structure was important and someone who had only ever wanted to impress people and fit in.

It turned out that public shaming *had* once been a process. A book of Delaware laws I discovered at the Massachusetts Historical Society revealed that if Jonah had been found guilty of "lying or publishing false news" in the 1800s, he would have been "fined, placed in the stocks for a period not exceeding four hours, or publicly whipped with not more than forty stripes." If the judge had chosen a whipping, local newspapers would have published a digest detailing the amount of squirming that had occurred. "Rash and Hayden squirmed considerably during the performance, and their backs were well-scarred," wrote the *Delawarean* of an 1876 whipping. If Jonah's whipper had been deemed to have not whipped hard enough, the reviews would have been scathing. "Suppressed remarks were expressed by large numbers. Many were heard to say that the punishment was a farce. Drunken fights and rows followed in rapid succession," reported Delaware's *Wilmington Daily Commercial* after a disappointing 1873 whipping.

The common assumption is that public punishments died out in the new great metropolises because they'd been judged useless. Everyone was too busy being industrious to bother to trail some transgressor through the city crowds like some volunteer scarlet letter. But according to the documents I found, that wasn't it at all. They didn't fizzle out because they were ineffective. They were stopped because they were far too brutal.

The movement against public shaming was already in full flow in March 1787 when Benjamin Rush, a United States founding father, wrote a paper calling for their outlawing— the stocks, the pillory, the whipping post, the lot.

Ignominy is universally acknowledged to be a worse punishment than death . . . It would seem strange that ignominy should ever have been adopted as a milder punishment than death, did we not know that the human mind seldom arrives at truth up on any subject till it has first reached the extremity of error.

—Benjamin Rush, "An Enquiry into the Effects
of Public Punishments Upon Criminals,
and Upon Society," March 9, 1787

In case you consider Rush too much of a bleeding-heart liberal, it's worth pointing out that his proposition for alternatives to public shaming included taking the criminal into a private room—away from the public gaze—and administering "bodily pain."

> To ascertain the nature, degrees, and duration of the bodily pain will require some knowledge of the principles of sensation and of the sympathies which occur in the nervous system.

Public punishments were abolished within fifty years of Rush's paper, with only Delaware weirdly holding out until 1952 (which is why the Delaware whipping critiques I excerpt were published in the 1870s).

The New York Times, baffled by Delaware's obstinacy, tried to argue the state into change in an 1867 editorial.

> If it had previously existed in [the convicted person's] bosom a spark of self-respect this exposure to public shame utterly extinguishes it. Without the hope that springs eternal in the human breast, without some desire to reform and become a good citizen, and the feeling that such a thing is possible, no criminal can ever return to honorable courses. The boy of eighteen who is whipped at New Castle [a Delaware whipping post] for larceny is in nine cases out of ten ruined. With his self-respect destroyed and the taunt and sneer of public disgrace branded upon his forehead, he feels himself lost and abandoned by his fellows.

> —QUOTED IN ROBERT GRAHAM CALDWELL,
> *Red Hannah: Delaware's Whipping Post*

As Jonah Lehrer stood in front of that giant-screen Twitter feed on February 12, 2013, he experienced something that had been widely considered appalling in the eighteenth century.

I left the Massachusetts Historical Society, took out my phone, and asked Twitter, "Has Twitter become a kangaroo court?"

"Not a kangaroo court," someone replied quite tersely. "Twitter still can't impose real sentences. Just commentary. Only unlike you, Jon, we aren't paid for it."

Was he right? It felt like a question that really needed answering because it didn't seem to be crossing any of our minds to wonder whether the person we had just shamed was okay or in ruins. I suppose that when shamings are delivered like remotely administered drone strikes nobody needs to think about how ferocious our collective power might be. The snowflake never needs to feel responsible for the avalanche.

● ● ●

Lehrer's intention in submitting himself to a public grilling was to show the world that he's ready to return to journalism, that we can trust him because he knows now not to trust himself. All he proved is that he's not wired like the rest of us. If he can figure out why that is, that would be a neuroscience story worth publishing.

—JEFF BERCOVICI, *Forbes*, FEBRUARY 12, 2013

I've been banging the drum for Lehrer to quiet his detrac-
tors and bank some goodwill by donating that $20,000 to
charity . . . Finally, I managed to get him on the phone this
afternoon. "I'm not interested in commenting," he told
me. Could he at least say whether he planned to keep the
money? "I read your article. I have nothing to say to you,"
he said, before hanging up.

—JEFF BERCOVICI, *Forbes*, FEBRUARY 13, 2013

"I'm still not entirely sure what I can give you . . ." Jonah
was talking to me on the phone from his home in Los Angeles.

"The twenty thousand dollars . . ." I said.

"It was absolutely a mistake," he said. "I didn't ask for it.
It was offered. They just gave it to me. I mean, what else do
you want? I . . ." Jonah paused. "Look, I got bills to pay. I
haven't earned a penny in seven months. I was flying high,
I was making lots of money. And all of a sudden you're making no money."

Jonah had finally agreed to a lengthier interview. He
sounded exhausted, like he'd been inside some spinning
machine designed by aliens to test the effects of stress on
humans. For a smart man, everything he'd done from the
moment Michael first e-mailed him had been a giant miscal-
culation. He'd been like a popped balloon shooting wildly in
all directions, lying frantically to Michael before slumping,
the air all gone, in the middle of one of the most terrible
shamings of our time.

"A friend forwarded me a blog post by Jerry Coyne from

the University of Chicago," Jonah said. "An eminent guy, I
interviewed him on occasion. He wrote a blog post about me
where he called me a sociopath."

> I sense that Lehrer is a bit of a sociopath. Yes, shows of
> contrition are often phony, meant to convince a gullible
> public (as in Lance Armstrong's case) that they're good to
> go again. But Lehrer can't even be bothered to fake an
> apology that sounds meaningful. Call me uncharitable,
> but if I were a magazine editor, I'd never hire him.
>
> —JERRY COYNE, QUOTED ON
> RICHARDBOWKER.COM, FEBRUARY 18, 2013

"I thought of you," Jonah said. "I thought, That's an interesting question for Jon. Jon's spent some time with me. Maybe
I *am* a sociopath."

The question didn't surprise me. Ever since I published a
book about psychopaths, people have been asking me if
they're one (or, if not them, their boss or their ex-boyfriend or
Lance Armstrong). Perhaps Jonah was honestly intrigued by
the possibility that he was one, but I didn't think so. I think
he knew he wasn't, and he had a different reason for wanting
to have this conversation. Academics shouldn't diagnose people from afar as sociopaths. It was a stupid thing for Jerry
Coyne to have done. I think Jonah wanted us to bitch about
his stupidity for a moment. It would be a way for him to re-
cover some self-esteem—to do a bit of shaming of someone
else. Jonah was at rock bottom, so I was happy to go along

with it. I told Jonah that he didn't seem like someone who had no conscience.

"Who the hell knows what a conscience is," Jonah replied. "If a conscience is living in a world defined by regrets, then, yeah, I've got a conscience. My very first thought every morning is what I've done wrong. That sounds self-pitying and I'd like you not to use that quote, but there's no other way around it."

"If it felt really important to use that quote, could I?" I asked him.

Jonah sighed. "I mean, it depends how you use it, but I'd prefer you not use it," he replied.

I use the quote here because it seems important, given that so many people imagine Jonah has some neurological lack of conscience.

"Regrets of the sort I have are all-consuming," Jonah continued. "I think about what I've done to the people I loved. What I've put my wife through. What I've put my brother through. What I've put my parents through. That is haunting. Long after I get over the loss of my status, and the loss of my career, which I enjoyed, I will never . . . Life is short. And I have caused tremendous pain to the people I love. I don't know what that feeling's called. Remorse sounds about right. There's a tremendous amount of remorse. And as time passes, that isn't going away. It is miserable and haunting."

I heard Jonah's daughter crying in the background. We talked about the "slippery slope" that led to the fake Dylan quotes. It began with the self-plagiarism—with Jonah reusing his own paragraphs in different stories. I told him I didn't consider that the crime of the century. "Frank Sinatra doesn't only sing 'My Way' once," I said.

"The self-plagiarism should have been a warning sign," Jonah said. "It should have been a sign that I was stretched. If I needed to recycle my own material, why was I bothering to write this blog post in the first place? Look, we can debate the ethics of it. And I've certainly heard lots of debate about this. But at the time I didn't think it was wrong. If I'd thought it was wrong, I would have taken some trouble to hide my tracks." He paused. "It should have been a huge flashing neon sign telling me, 'You are getting careless.' You're taking shortcuts and not noticing, and shortcuts become habits, and you excuse them because you're too busy. I wasn't turning anything down."

"What would have been wrong with turning things down?" I asked.

"It was some toxic mixture of insecurity and ambition," said Jonah. "I always felt like a fad. I felt like I was going to be hot for a second and then I would disappear. So I had to act while I could. And there was just some deep-seated . . . I sound like I'm on a couch with my shrink . . . some very dangerous and reckless ambition. You combine insecurity and ambition, and you get an inability to say no to things. And then one day you get an e-mail saying there's these four [six] Dylan quotes, and they can't be explained, and they can't be found anywhere else, and you realize you made them up in your book proposal three years before, and you were too lazy, too stupid, to ever check. I can only wish, and I wish this profoundly, I'd had the temerity, the courage, to do a fact check on my last book. But as anyone who does a fact check knows, they're not particularly fun things to go through. Your story gets a little flatter. You're forced to grapple with all your mistakes, conscious and unconscious . . ."

"So you forgot that the fake quotes were in the book?" I asked Jonah.

"*Forget* gets me off the hook too easily," he replied. "I didn't want to remember. So I made no effort to. I wrote well. So why check?"

"So you were sloppy?"

"I don't want to just blame sloppiness," he said. "It was sloppiness and deception. Sloppiness and lies. I lied to cover up the sloppiness."

I'd been thinking that when I told Jonah his speech was fantastic it was probably a bad steer. In truth, I'd needed to read it three or four times on the plane because the words kept swirling around on the page, and I didn't know whether that was a reflection of attention deficiency on my part or abstruse phrasing on Jonah's. But like all journalists, I really love a scoop—a scoop keeps at bay the scream of failure—and I thought that telling him it was fantastic was my best chance of winning the interview.

"I worked really hard on it," Jonah said. "I was looking at the Twitter stream during it and the things people were saying . . . Some people saw the FBI analogies as the worst possible thing in the world. But that's not some deceptive trick. That's the way I make sense of the world. That's how I think. Clearly it was a mistake. But . . ."

"That Twitter stream!" I said.

"I was trying to apologize, and to see the response to it live . . . I didn't know if I was going to get through that. I had to turn off some emotional switch in me. I think I had to shut down."

"What are the tweets you remember most?"

"It wasn't the totally off-the-wall cruel ones, because those are so easy to discount," he said. "It's the ones that mixed in a little tenderness with the shiv."

"Like what?"

"I don't want to . . ."

Jonah said he couldn't judge why people "got so mad" about his apology. I said I thought it was because it sounded too much like a Jonah Lehrer speech from the old days. People wanted to see him altered somehow. His not being overtly cowed gave the audience permission to envisage him dramatically, a monster immune to shame.

"They didn't want you to intellectualize it," I said. "They wanted you to be emotional. If you'd been more emotional, they'd have gone for it more."

Jonah sighed. "That may have been a better strategy," he said. "But it wasn't a strategy I wanted to rehearse onstage. It was not something I wanted to share with the universe, with everyone on Twitter. I didn't want to talk about how this had ruined me. That's something for me to deal with, and for my loved ones to help me through. But that's not something I wanted to get up onstage in front of the Internet and talk about."

"Why not?" I asked.

"Oh, gosh, I don't know," said Jonah. "Could you do that?"

"Yes," I said. "I think I could. And I think that would mean I'd survive better than you."

"So what would Jon Ronson's apology speech be?" Jonah said. "What would you say?"

"Right," I said. "I'd say . . . okay . . . I . . . Hello. I'm Jon Ronson and I want to apologize for . . ." What *would* I say? I cleared my throat. "I just want everyone to know that I'm really upset . . ." Jonah was listening patiently on the line. I stopped. Even though I was just play-acting, I felt wiped out. And I hadn't really even got anywhere in my attempt.

"What happened to you is my worst nightmare," I said.

"Yeah," Jonah replied. "It was mine too."

. . .

Four more months passed. The winter became the early summer. Then, unexpectedly, Andrew Wylie began shopping a new Jonah Lehrer book proposal around New York City's publishers. *A Book About Love.* The proposal was immediately leaked to *The New York Times.* In it Jonah described the moment he felt "the shiver of a voice mail message."

I have been found out. I puke into a recycling bin. And then I start to cry. Why was I crying? I had been caught in a lie, a desperate attempt to conceal my mistakes. And now it was clear that, within 24 hours, my fall would begin. I would lose my job and my reputation. My private shame would become public.

Jonah then described leaving St. Louis and returning to Los Angeles, his suit and shirt "stained with sweat and vomit."

I open the front door and take off my dirty shirt and weep on the shoulder of my wife. My wife is caring but confused: How the hell could I be so reckless? I have no good answers.

—JONAH LEHRER'S BOOK PROPOSAL, AS LEAKED TO
The New York Times, JUNE 6, 2013

The New York media community declared itself resolutely indifferent to Jonah's suffering. " 'Recycling bin' is a hilarious choice of detail for the compulsive plagiarist," wrote *Gawker*'s Tom Scocca. "And, obviously: Bring us two witnesses who saw you puke when and where you claim you puked. Or don't bother."

And then, to my amazement, *Slate*'s Daniel Engber announced that he had spent a day combing through Jonah's proposal and believed he had uncovered plagiarism within it.

Surely Jonah hadn't been that insanely reckless?

When I read Engber's article closer, things didn't seem quite so clear-cut. "A chapter on the secret to having a happy marriage," Engber writes, "comes close to copying a recent essay on the same subject by Adam Gopnik, Lehrer's onetime colleague at *The New Yorker*."

Gopnik: In 1838, when Darwin was first thinking of marriage, he made an irresistible series of notes on the subject—a scientific-seeming list of marriage pros and cons . . . In favor of marriage, he included the acquisition of a "constant companion and friend in old age" and, memorably and conclusively, decided that a wife would be "better than a dog, anyhow."

Lehrer: In July 1838, Charles Darwin considered the possibility of marriage in his scientific notebook. His thoughts quickly took the shape of a list, a balance sheet of reasons to "marry" and "not marry." The pros of wedlock were straightforward: Darwin cited the possibility of children ("if it please God"), the health benefits of attachment and the pleasure of having a "constant companion (& friend in old age)." A wife, he wrote, was probably "better than a dog anyhow."

Gopnik: And the Darwins went on to have something close to an ideal marriage.

Lehrer: This might seem like an inauspicious start to a relationship, but the Darwins went on to have a nearly ideal marriage.

And so on, for a few paragraphs. Engber wasn't totally sure this counted as plagiarism, "or if [Lehrer] modified his words to stop just short of doing so." Or maybe both men had drawn from the same source: "In the footnotes Lehrer cites page 661 of Desmond and Moore's 1991 biography of Darwin. Anyone who has a copy of that book is invited to check the wordings."

But even if it wasn't plagiarism, Engber was "convinced that Lehrer hasn't changed his ways at all. He's set his course as clearly as can be. He'll recycle and repeat, he'll puke his gritty guts out."

No matter what transgressions Jonah had or hadn't committed—it seemed to me—he couldn't win. But his *Book About Love* is scheduled to be published by Simon & Schuster around the same time that this book will appear, so we'll all learn at once if it will win him some redemption.

Four

God That Was Awesome

During the months that followed, it became routine. Everyday people, some with young children, were getting annihilated for tweeting some badly worded joke to their hundred or so followers. I'd meet them in restaurants and airport cafés—spectral figures wandering the earth like the living dead in the business wear of their former lives. It was happening with such regularity that it didn't even seem coincidental that one of them, Justine Sacco, had been working in the same office building as Michael Moynihan until three weeks earlier when, passing through Heathrow Airport, she wrote a tweet that came out badly.

It was December 20, 2013. For the previous two days she'd been tweeting little acerbic jokes to her 170 followers about her holiday travels. She was like a social media Sally Bowles, decadent and flighty and unaware that serious politics were looming. There was her joke about the German man on the plane from New York: "*Weird German Dude: You're in first class. It's 2014. Get some deodorant.—Inner monolog as I inhale BO. Thank god for pharmaceuticals.*" Then the layover at Heathrow: "*Chili—cucumber sandwiches—bad teeth. Back in London!*" Then the final leg: "*Going to Africa. Hope I don't get AIDS. Just kidding. I'm white!*"

She chuckled to herself, pressed send, and wandered around the airport for half an hour, sporadically checking Twitter.

"I got nothing," she told me. "No replies."

I imagined her feeling a bit deflated about this—that sad feeling when nobody congratulates you for being funny, that black silence when the Internet doesn't talk back. She boarded the plane. It was an eleven-hour flight. She slept. When the plane landed, she turned on her phone. Straightaway there was a text from someone she hadn't spoken to since high school: "*I'm so sorry to see what's happening.*"

She looked at it, baffled.

"And then my phone started to explode," she said.

We were having this conversation three weeks later at—her choice of location—the Cookshop restaurant in New York

City. It was the very same restaurant where Michael had recounted to me the tale of Jonah's destruction. It was becoming for me the Restaurant of Stories of Obliterated Lives. But it was only a half coincidence. It was close to the building where they both worked. Michael had been offered a job at *The Daily Beast* as a result of his great Jonah scoop, and Justine had an office upstairs, running the PR department for the magazine's publisher, IAC—which also owned Vimeo and OkCupid and Match.com. The reason why she wanted to meet me here, and why she was wearing her expensive-looking work clothes, was that at six p.m. she was due in there to clean out her desk.

As she sat on the runway at Cape Town Airport, a second text popped up: *"You need to call me immediately."* It was from her best friend, Hannah. *"You're the number one worldwide trend on Twitter right now."*

"In light of @JustineSacco disgusting racist tweet, I'm donating to @CARE today," and "How did @JustineSacco get a PR job?! Her level of racist ignorance belongs on Fox News. #AIDS can affect anyone!" and "No words for that horribly disgusting, racist as fuck tweet from Justine Sacco. I am beyond horrified," and "I'm an IAC employee and I don't want @JustineSacco doing any communications on our behalf ever again. Ever," and "Everyone go report this cunt @Justine Sacco," and from IAC: "This is an outrageous, offensive comment. Employee in question currently unreachable on an intl flight," and "Fascinated by the @JustineSacco train wreck. It's global and she's apparently *still on the plane,*" and "All I want for Christmas is to see @JustineSacco's face when her plane lands and she checks her inbox/voicemail," and "Oh man, @JustineSacco is going to have the most painful phone-turning-on moment ever when her plane lands," and "Looks like @JustineSacco lands in about 9mins, this should be interesting," and "We are about to watch this @JustineSacco bitch get fired. In REAL time. Before she even KNOWS she's getting fired," and then, after Hannah frantically deleted Justine's Twitter account, "Sorry @JustineSacco—your tweet lives on forever," and so on for a total of a hundred thousand tweets, according to calculations by the website BuzzFeed, until weeks later: "Man, remember Justine Sacco? #HasJustine LandedYet. God that was awesome. MILLIONS of people waiting for her to land."

I once asked a car-crash victim what it had felt like to be in a smashup. She said her eeriest memory was how one second the car was her friend, working for her, its contours designed to fit her body perfectly, everything smooth and sleek and luxurious, and then a blink of an eye later it had become a jagged weapon of torture—like she was inside an iron maiden. Her friend had become her worst enemy.

Over the years, I've sat across tables from a lot of people whose lives had been destroyed. Usually, the people who did the destroying were the government or the military or big business or, as with Jonah Lehrer, basically themselves (at least at first with Jonah—we took over as he tried to apologize). Justine Sacco felt like the first person I had ever interviewed who had been destroyed by *us*.

• • •

Google has an engine—Google AdWords—that tells you how many times your name has been searched for during any given month. In October 2013, Justine was googled thirty times. In November 2013, she was googled thirty times. Between December 20 and the end of December, she was googled 1,220,000 times.

A man had been waiting for her at Cape Town Airport. He was a Twitter user, @Zac_R. He took her photograph and

Justine Sacco (in dark glasses) at Cape
Town Airport. Photograph by @Zac_R,
reproduced with his permission.

posted it online. "Yup," he wrote, "@JustineSacco HAS in fact landed at Cape Town international. She's decided to wear sunnies as a disguise."

Three weeks had passed since Justine had pressed send on the tweet. The *New York Post* had been following her to the gym. Newspapers were ransacking her Twitter feed for more horrors.

> And the award for classiest tweet of all time goes to . . .
>   "I had a sex dream about an autistic kid last night." (February 24, 2012)
>
> —"16 Tweets Justine Sacco Regrets,"
> BuzzFeed, December 20, 2013

This was the only time Justine would ever talk to a journalist about what happened to her, she told me. It was just too harrowing. And inadvisable. "As a publicist," she e-mailed, "I don't know that I would ever recommend to a client that they participate in your book. I'm very nervous about it. I am really terrified about opening myself up to future attacks. But I think it's necessary. I want someone to just show how crazy my situation is."

It was crazy because "only an *insane* person would think that white people don't get AIDS." That was about the first thing she said to me when she sat down. "To me, it was so insane a comment for an American to make I thought there was no way that anyone could possibly think it was a literal statement. I know there are hateful people out there who don't like other people and are generally mean. But that's not me."

Justine had been about three hours into her flight—probably asleep in the air above Spain or Algeria—when retweets of her tweet began to overwhelm my Twitter feed. After an initial happy little "Oh, wow, someone is *fucked*," I started to think her shamers must have been gripped by some kind of group madness or something. It seemed obvious that her tweet, whilst not a great joke, wasn't racist, but a reflexive comment on white privilege—on our tendency to naively imagine ourselves immune from life's horrors. Wasn't it?

"It was a joke about a situation that exists," Justine e-mailed. "It was a joke about a dire situation that does exist in post-apartheid South Africa that we don't pay attention to. It was completely outrageous commentary on the disproportionate AIDS statistics. Unfortunately, I am not a character on *South Park* or a comedian, so I had no business commenting on the epidemic in such a politically incorrect manner on a public platform. To put it simply, I wasn't trying to raise awareness of AIDS, or piss off the world, or ruin my life. Living in America puts us in a bit of a bubble when it comes to what is going on in the third world. I was making fun of that bubble."

As it happens, I once made a similar—albeit funnier—joke in a column for *The Guardian*. It was about a time when I flew into the United States and was sent for "secondary processing" (there was a mafioso hit man on the run at the time with a name that apparently sounded quite a lot like Jon Ronson). I was taken into a packed holding room and told to wait.

There are signs everywhere saying: "The use of cell phones is strictly prohibited."
I'm sure they won't mind *me* checking my text messages, I think. I mean, after all, I *am* white.

My joke was funnier than Justine's joke. It was better worded. Plus, as it didn't invoke AIDS sufferers, it was less unpleasant. So mine was funnier, better worded, and less unpleasant. But it suddenly felt like that Russian roulette scene in *The Deer Hunter* when Christopher Walken puts the gun to his head and lets out a scream and pulls the trigger and the gun doesn't go off. It was to a large extent Justine's own fault that so many people thought she was a racist. Her reflexive sarcasm had been badly worded, her wider Twitter persona quite brittle. But I hadn't needed to think about her tweet for more than a few seconds before I understood what she'd been trying to say. There must have been among her shamers a lot of people who chose to willfully misunderstand it for some reason.

"I can't fully grasp the misconception that's happening around the world," Justine said. "They've taken my name and my picture, and have created this Justine Sacco that's not me and have labeled this person a racist. I have this fear that if I were in a car accident tomorrow and lost my memory and came back and googled myself, that would be my new reality."

I suddenly remembered how weirdly tarnished I felt when the spambot men created their fake Jon Ronson, getting my character traits all wrong, turning me into some horrific, garrulous foodie, and strangers believed it was me, and there was nothing I could do. That's what was happening to Justine, although instead of a foodie she was a racist and instead of fifty people it was 1,220,000.

Journalists are supposed to be intrepid. We're supposed to stand tall in the face of injustice and not fear crazy mobs. But neither Justine nor I saw much fearlessness in how her story was reported. Even articles about how "we could all be minutes away from having a Justine Sacco moment" were all couched in "I am *NO WAY* defending what she said," she told me.

But as vile as the sentiment she expressed was, there are some potential extenuating circumstances here that don't excuse her behavior but might mitigate her misdeed somewhat. Repugnant as her joke was, there is a difference between outright hate speech and even the most ill-advised attempt at humor.

—ANDREW WALLENSTEIN, "JUSTINE SACCO: SYMPATHY FOR THIS TWITTER DEVIL," *Variety*, DECEMBER 22, 2013

Andrew Wallenstein was braver than most. But still: It read like the old media saying to social media, "Don't hurt me."

Justine released an apology statement. She cut short her South African family vacation "because of safety concerns. People were threatening to go on strike at the hotels I was booked into if I showed up. I was told no one could guarantee my safety." Word spread around the Internet that she was heiress to a $4.8 billion fortune, as people assumed her father was the South African mining tycoon Desmond Sacco. I wrongly thought this was true about her right up until I alluded to her billions over lunch and she looked at me like I was crazy.

"I grew up on Long Island," she said.

"Not in a Jay Gatsby–type estate?" I said.

"Not in a Jay Gatsby–type estate," Justine said. "My mom was single my entire life. She was a flight attendant. My dad sold carpets."

(She later e-mailed that while she "grew up with a single mom who was a flight attendant and worked two jobs, when I was twenty-one or twenty-two, she married well. My stepfather is pretty well off, and I think there was a picture of my mom's car on my Instagram, which gave the impression that I'm from a wealthy family. So maybe that's another reason why people assumed I was a spoiled brat. I don't know. But thought it was worth bringing up to you.")

Years ago I interviewed some white supremacists from an Aryan Nations compound in Idaho about their conviction that the Bilderberg Group—a secretive annual meeting of politicians and business leaders—was a Jewish conspiracy.

"How can you call it a Jewish conspiracy when practically no Jews go to it?" I asked them.

"They may not be actual Jews," one replied, "but they are . . ." He paused. ". . . Jewish."

So there it was: At Aryan Nations, you didn't need to be an actual Jew to be Jew-*ish*. And the same was true on Twitter with the privileged racist Justine Sacco, who was neither especially privileged nor a racist. But it didn't matter. It was enough that it sort of seemed like she was.

Her extended family in South Africa were ANC supporters. One of the first things Justine's aunt told her when she arrived at the family home from Cape Town Airport was: "This is not what our family stands for. And now, by association, you've almost tarnished the family."

At this, Justine started to cry. I sat looking at her for a moment. Then I tried to say something hopeful to improve the mood.

"Sometimes things need to reach a brutal nadir before people see sense," I said. "So maybe you're our brutal nadir."

"Wow," Justine said. She dried her eyes. "Of all the things I could have been in society's collective consciousness, it never struck me that I'd end up a brutal nadir."

A woman approached our table—a friend of Justine's. She sat down next to her, fixed her with an empathetic look, and said something at such a low volume I couldn't hear it.

"Oh, you think I'm going to be *grateful* for this?" Justine replied.

"Yes, you will," the woman said. "Every step prepares you for the next, especially when you don't think so. I know you can't see that right now. That's okay. I get it. But come on. Did you really have your *dream job*?"

Justine looked at her. "I think I did," she said.

. . .

I got an e-mail from the *Gawker* journalist Sam Biddle—the man who may have started the onslaught against Justine. One of Justine's 170 followers had sent him the tweet. He retweeted it to his 15,000 followers. And that's how it may have begun.

"The fact that she was a PR chief made it delicious," he e-mailed me. "It's satisfying to be able to say 'OK, let's make a racist tweet by a senior IAC employee count this time.' And it did. I'd do it again."

Her destruction was justified, Sam Biddle was saying, because Justine was a racist, and because attacking her was punching up. They were cutting down a member of the media elite, continuing the civil rights tradition that started with Rosa Parks, the hitherto silenced underdogs shaming into submission the powerful racist. But I didn't think any of those things were true. If punching Justine Sacco was ever punching up—and it didn't seem so to me given that she was an unknown PR woman with 170 Twitter followers—the punching only intensified as she plummeted to the ground. Punching Jonah Lehrer wasn't punching up either—not when he was begging for forgiveness in front of that giant-screen Twitter feed.

A life had been ruined. What was it for: just some social media drama? I think our natural disposition as humans is to plod along until we get old and stop. But with social media, we've created a stage for constant artificial high drama. Every day a new person emerges as a magnificent hero or a sickening villain. It's all very sweeping, and not the way we actually are as people. What rush was overpowering us at times like this? What were we getting out of it?

I could tell Sam Biddle was finding it startling too—like when you shoot a gun and the power of it sends you recoiling violently backward. He said he was "surprised" to see how quickly Justine was destroyed: "I never wake up and hope I get to fire someone that day—and certainly never hope to ruin anyone's life." Still, his e-mail ended, he had a feeling she'd be "fine eventually, if not already. Everyone's attention span is so short. They'll be mad about something new today."

.   .   .

When Justine left me that evening to clear out her desk, she got only as far as the lobby of her office building before she collapsed on the floor in tears. Later, we talked again. I told her what Sam Biddle had said—about how she was "probably fine now." I was sure he wasn't being deliberately glib. He was just like everyone who participates in mass online destruction. Who would want to know? Whatever that pleasurable rush that overwhelms us is—group madness or something else—nobody wants to ruin it by facing the fact that it comes with a cost.

"Well, I'm not fine," Justine said. "I'm really suffering. I had a great career and I loved my job and it was taken away from me and there was a lot of glory in that. Everybody else was very *happy* about that. I cried out my body weight in the first twenty-four hours. It was incredibly traumatic. You don't sleep. You wake up in the middle of the night forgetting where you are. All of a sudden you don't know what you're supposed to do. You've got no schedule. You've got no"—she paused—"purpose. I'm thirty years old. I had a great career. If I don't have a plan, if I don't start making steps to reclaim my identity and remind myself of who I am on a daily basis, then I might lose myself. I'm single. So it's not like I can date, because we google everyone we might date. So that's been taken away from me too. How am I going to meet new people? What are they going to think of me?"

She asked me who else was going to be in my book about people who had been publicly shamed.

"Well, Jonah Lehrer so far," I said.

"How's he doing?" she asked me.

"Pretty badly, I think," I said.

"Badly in what way?" She looked concerned—I think more for what this might prophesy about her own future than about Jonah's.

"I think he's broken," I said.

"When you say Jonah seems broken, what do you mean?" Justine said.

"I think he's broken and that people mistake it for shamelessness," I said.

People really were very keen to imagine Jonah as shameless, as lacking in that quality, like he was something not quite human that had adopted human form. I suppose it's no surprise that we feel the need to dehumanize the people we hurt—before, during, or after the hurting occurs. But it always comes as a surprise. In psychology it's known as cognitive dissonance. It's the idea that it feels stressful and painful for us to hold two contradictory ideas at the same time (like the idea that we're kind people and the idea that we've just destroyed someone). And so to ease the pain we create illusory ways to justify our contradictory behavior. It's like when I used to smoke and I'd hope the tobacconist would hand me the pack that read SMOKING CAUSES AGING OF THE SKIN instead of the pack that read SMOKING KILLS—because aging of the skin? I didn't mind *that*.

Justine and I agreed to meet again, but not for months, she told me. We'd meet again in five months. She was compelled to make sure that this was not her narrative. "I can't just sit at home and watch movies every day and cry and feel sorry for myself," she said. I think Justine wasn't thrilled to be included in the same book as Jonah. She didn't see herself as being anything like Jonah. Jonah lied repeatedly, again and again. How could Jonah bounce back when he'd sacrificed his character and lied to millions? Justine had to believe that there was a stark difference between that and her making a tasteless joke. She did something stupid, but she didn't trash her integrity.

She couldn't bear the thought of being preserved within the pages of my book as a sad case. She needed to avoid falling into depression and self-loathing. She knew that the next five months were going to be crucial for her. She was determined to show the people who had smashed her up that she could rise again.

How could she tell her story, she thought, when it was just beginning?

. . .

The day after my lunch with Justine, I caught the train to Washington, D.C., to meet someone I had prejudged as a frightening man—a fearsome American narcissist—Ted Poe. For the twenty or so years he was a judge in Houston, Poe's nationally famous trademark was to publicly shame defendants in the showiest ways he could dream up, "using citizens as virtual props in his personal theater of the absurd," as the legal writer Jonathan Turley once put it.

Given society's intensifying eagerness to publicly shame people, I wanted to meet someone who had been doing it professionally for decades. What would today's citizen shamers think of Ted Poe—his personality and his motivations—now that they were basically becoming him? What impact had his shaming frenzy had on the world around him—on the wrongdoers and the bystanders and himself?

Ted Poe's punishments were sometimes zany—ordering petty criminals to shovel manure, etc.—and sometimes as ingenious as a Goya painting. Like the one he handed down to a Houston teenager, Mike Hubacek. In 1996, Hubacek had been driving drunk at one hundred miles per hour with no headlights. He crashed into a van carrying a married couple and their nanny. The husband and the nanny were killed. Poe sentenced Hubacek to 110 days of boot camp, and to carry a sign once a month for ten years in front of high schools and bars that read I KILLED TWO PEOPLE WHILE DRIVING DRUNK, and to erect a cross and a Star of David at the scene of the crash site, and to keep it maintained, and to keep photographs of the victims in his wallet for ten years, and to send ten dollars every week for ten years to a memorial fund in the names of the victims, and to observe the autopsy of a person killed in a drunk-driving accident.

Punishments like these had proved too psychologically torturous for other people. In 1982 a seventeen-year-old boy named Kevin Tunell had killed a girl, Susan Herzog, while driving drunk near Washington, D.C. Her parents sued him and were awarded $1.5 million in damages. But they offered the boy a deal. They would reduce the fine to just $936 if he'd mail them a check for $1, made out in Susan's name, every Friday for eighteen years. He gratefully accepted their offer.

Years later, the boy began missing payments, and when Susan's parents took him to court, he broke down. Every time he filled in her name, he said, the guilt would tear him apart: "It hurts too much," he said. He tried to give the Herzogs two boxes of prewritten checks, dated one per week until the end of 2001, a year longer than was required. But they refused to take them.

Judge Ted Poe's critics—like the civil rights group the ACLU—argued to him the dangers of these ostentatious punishments, especially those that were carried out in public. They said it was no coincidence that public shaming had enjoyed such a renaissance in Mao's China and Hitler's Germany and the Ku Klux Klan's America—it destroys souls, brutalizing everyone, the onlookers included, dehumanizing them as much as the person being shamed. How could Poe take people with such low self-esteem that they needed to, say, rob a store, and then hold them up to officially sanctioned public ridicule?

But Poe brushed the criticisms off. Criminals didn't have *low* self-esteem, he argued. It was quite the opposite. "The people I see have *too good* a self-esteem," he told *The Boston Globe* in 1997. "Some folks say everyone should have high self-esteem, but sometimes people *should* feel bad."

Poe's shaming methods were so admired in Houston society that he ended up getting elected to Congress as the representative for Texas's Second Congressional District. He is currently Congress's "top talker," according to the *Los Angeles Times*, having made 431 speeches between 2009 and 2011, against abortion, illegal immigrants, socialized health care, and so on. He always ends them with his catchphrase: "And that's just the way it is!"

"It wasn't the 'theater of the absurd.'" Ted Poe sat opposite me in his office in the Rayburn House Office Building in Washington, D.C. I'd just quoted to him his critic Jonathan Turley's line—"using citizens as virtual props in his personal theater of the absurd"—and he was bristling. He wore cowboy boots with his suit—another Poe trademark, like the catchphrase and the shaming. He had the look and mannerisms of his friend George W. Bush. "It was the theater of the *different*," he said.

The Rayburn building is where all the congressmen and congresswomen have their offices. Each office door is decorated with the state flag of the congressperson who is inside:

the bald eagles of Illinois and North Dakota and the bear of California and the horse's head of New Jersey and the strange bleeding pelican of Louisiana. Poe's office is staffed by handsome, serious-looking Texas men and tough, pretty Texas women who were extremely nice to me but totally ignored all my subsequent e-mail requests for clarifications and follow-up interviews. Although Poe ended the interview by warmly shaking my hand, I suspect that the moment I left the room he told his staff, "That man was an idiot. Ignore all future e-mail requests from him."

He recounted to me some of his favorite shamings: "Like the young man who loved the thrill of stealing. I could have put him in jail. But I decided that he had to carry a sign for seven days: I STOLE FROM THIS STORE. DON'T BE A THIEF OR THIS COULD BE YOU. He was supervised. We worked all the security out. I got that down to an art for those people who worried about security. At the end of the week the store manager called me: 'All week I didn't have any stealing going on in the store!' The store manager loved it."

"But aren't you turning the criminal justice system into entertainment?" I said.

"Ask the guy out there," Ted Poe replied. "He doesn't think he's entertaining anybody."

"I don't mean him," I said. "I mean the effect it has on the people watching."

"The public liked it." Poe nodded. "People stopped and talked to him about his conduct. One lady wanted to take him to church on Sunday and save him! She *did!*" Poe let out a big high-pitched Texas laugh. "She said, 'Come with me, you poor thing!' End of the week, I brought him back into court. He said it was the most embarrassing thing that had ever happened to him. It changed his conduct. Eventually, he got a bachelor's degree. He's got a business in Houston now." Poe paused. "I have put my share of folks in the penitentiary. Sixty-six percent of them go back to prison. Eighty-five percent of those people we publicly shamed we never saw again. It was too embarrassing for them the first time. It wasn't the 'theater of the absurd,' it was the theater of the *effective*. It worked."

Poe was being annoyingly convincing, even though he later admitted to me that his recidivism argument was a misleading one. Poe was far more likely to sentence a first-time offender—someone who was already feeling scared and remorseful and determined to change—to a shaming. But even so, I was learning something about public shaming today that I hadn't anticipated at all.

It had started earlier that morning in my hotel room when I telephoned Mike Hubacek, the teenager who had killed two people while driving drunk in 1996. I had wanted him to describe the feeling of being forced to walk up and down the side of the road holding a placard that read I KILLED TWO PEOPLE WHILE DRIVING DRUNK. But first we talked about the crash. He told me he spent the first six months after it happened lying in his prison cell, replaying it over and over.

"What images did you replay?" I asked him.

"None," he replied. "I had completely blacked out during it and I don't remember anything. But I thought about it daily. I still do. It's a part of me. I suffered a lot of survivor's guilt. At the time, I almost convinced myself I was in a living purgatory. I lived to suffer. I went more than a year and a half without looking in a mirror. You learn to shave using your hand as a guide."

Being in purgatory, he said, he had resigned himself to a lifetime of incarceration. But then Ted Poe unexpectedly pulled him out. And he suddenly found himself walking up and down the side of the road holding that placard.

And there on the side of the road, he said, he understood that there was a use for him. He could basically become a living placard that warned people against driving drunk. And so nowadays he lectures in schools about the dangers. He owns a halfway house—Sober Living Houston. And he credits Judge Ted Poe for it all.

"I'm forever grateful to him," he said.

My trip to Washington, D.C., wasn't turning out how I'd hoped. I'd assumed that Ted Poe would be such a terrible person and negative role model that the social media shamers would realize with horror that this was what they were becoming and vow to change their ways. But Mike Hubacek thought his shaming was the best thing that had ever happened to him. This was especially true, he told me, because the onlookers had been so nice. He'd feared abuse and ridicule. But no. "Ninety percent of the responses on the street were 'God bless you' and 'Things will be okay,'" he said. Their kindness meant everything, he said. It made it all right. It set him on his path to salvation.

"Social media shamings are *worse* than your shamings," I suddenly said to Ted Poe.

He looked taken aback. "They *are* worse," he replied. "They're anonymous."

"Or even if they're not anonymous, it's such a pile-on they may as well be," I said.

"They're *brutal*," he said.

I suddenly became aware that throughout our conversation I'd been using the word *they*. And each time I did, it felt like I was being spineless. The fact was, *they* weren't brutal. *We* were brutal.

In the early days of Twitter there were no shamings. We were Eve in the Garden of Eden. We chatted away unself-consciously. As somebody back then wrote, "Facebook is where you lie to your friends, Twitter is where you tell the truth to strangers." Having funny and honest conversations with like-minded people I didn't know got me through hard times that were unfolding in my actual house. Then came the Jan Moir and the LA Fitness shamings—shamings to be proud of—and I remember how exciting it felt when hitherto remote evil billionaires like Rupert Murdoch and Donald Trump created their own Twitter accounts. For the first time in history we sort of had direct access to ivory-tower oligarchs like them. We became keenly watchful for transgressions.

After a while, it wasn't just transgressions we were keenly watchful for. It was misspeakings. Fury at the terribleness of other people had started to consume us a lot. And the rage that swirled around seemed increasingly in disproportion to whatever stupid thing some celebrity had said. It felt different to satire or journalism or criticism. It felt like punishment. In fact, it felt weird and empty when there *wasn't* anyone to be furious about. The days between shamings felt like days picking at fingernails, treading water.

I'd been dismayed by the cruelty of the people who tore Jonah apart as he tried to apologize. But *they* weren't the mob. *We* were the mob. I'd been blithely doing the same thing for a year or more. I had drifted into a new way of being. Who were the victims of my shamings? I could barely remember. I had only the vaguest recollection of the people I'd piled onto and what terrible things they'd done to deserve it.

This is partly because my memory has degenerated badly these past years. In fact, I was recently at a spa—my wife booked it for me as a special surprise, which shows she really doesn't know me because I don't like being touched—and as I lay on the massage table, the conversation turned to my bad memory.

"I can hardly remember anything about my childhood!" I told the masseur. "It's all gone!"

"A lot of people who can't remember their childhoods," she replied, as she massaged my shoulders, "it turns out that they were sexually abused. By their parents."

"Well, I'd remember *THAT*," I said.

But it wasn't just the fault of my lousy memory. It was the sheer volume of transgressors I'd chastised. How could I commit to memory that many people? Well, there were the spambot men. For a second in Poe's office I reminisced fondly on the moment someone suggested we gas the cunts. That had given me such a good feeling that it felt a shame to interrogate it—to question why it had beguiled me so.

"The justice system in the West has a lot of problems," Poe said, "but at least there are rules. You have basic rights as the accused. You have your day in court. You don't have any rights when you're accused on the Internet. And the consequences are worse. It's worldwide forever."

It felt good to see the balance of power shift so that someone like Ted Poe was afraid of people like us. But he wouldn't sentence people to hold a placard for something they hadn't been convicted of. He wouldn't sentence someone for telling a joke that came out badly. The people we were destroying were no longer just people like Jonah: public figures who had committed actual transgressions. They were private individuals who really hadn't done anything much wrong. Ordinary humans were being forced to learn damage control, like corporations that had committed PR disasters. It was very stressful.

"We are *more frightening than you*," I said to Poe, feeling quite awed.

Poe sat back in his chair, satisfied. "You are much more frightening," he said. "You are much more frightening."

We were much more frightening than Judge Ted Poe. The powerful, crazy, cruel people I usually write about tend to be in far-off places. The powerful, crazy, cruel people were now us.

It felt like we were soldiers making war on other people's flaws, and there had suddenly been an escalation in hostilities.

Five

Man Descends Several Rungs in the Ladder of Civilization

Group madness. Was that the explanation for our shaming frenzy, our escalating war on flaws? It's an idea that gets invoked by social scientists whenever a crowd becomes frightening. Take the London riots of August 2011. The violence had begun with police shooting to death a Tottenham man, Mark Duggan. A protest followed, which turned into five days of rioting and looting. The rioters were in Camden

Town, a mile from my house, smashing up kebab shops and JJB Sports, Dixons, and Vodafone stores. Then they were in Kentish Town, half a mile down the hill from us. We frantically locked our doors and stared in horror at the TV news. The crowd had become contaminated—according to Dr. Gary Slutkin, an epidemiologist writing in *The Observer*— by a virus that infects the mind and causes a "collective communal group-think-motivated violence." (Here Slutkin was quoting the cognitive psychologist Aaron Beck.) It sounded like a zombie film. In *The Guardian*, Jack Levin—a professor of sociology and criminology at Northeastern University in Boston—called the riots "the violent version of the Mexican wave." People were infected with "emotional contagion. It is a feature of every riot . . . People get together in a group and commit acts of violence that they would never dream of committing individually."

Luckily, the rioting fizzled out at the bottom of our hill that night. Which, now that I thought about it, didn't sound like the violent version of the Mexican wave at all. If the rioters had really lost their minds to a horrifying virus, you'd think they would have carried on up the hill. Our hill, Highgate West Hill, is very steep—one of the steepest in London. I think the rioters made the extremely lucid decision not to climb it.

It turns out that the concept of group madness was the creation of a nineteenth-century French doctor called Gustave LeBon. His idea was that humans totally lose control of their behavior in a crowd. Our free will evaporates. A contagious madness takes over, a complete lack of restraint. We can't stop ourselves. So we riot, or we jubilantly tear down Justine Sacco.

It wasn't easy to learn about Gustave LeBon. For being the father of such an enduring theory, almost nothing has been written about him. Only one man has ever tried to piece his life story together—Bob Nye, a professor of European intellectual history at Oregon State University.

"LeBon was from a provincial town in the west of France," he told me over the telephone. "But he decided he wanted to go to medical school in Paris."

This was a France so wary of the crowd that in 1853, when LeBon was twelve, Napoleon III commissioned the town planner Georges-Eugène Haussmann to demolish Paris's twisted medieval streets and build long wide boulevards instead—urban planning as crowd control. It didn't work. In 1871 Parisian workers rose up in protest against their conditions. They took hostages—local bureaucrats and police officers—who were summarily tried and executed. The government fled to Versailles.

LeBon was a great admirer of the Parisian elite (even though the Parisian elite didn't seem in the slightest bit interested in him—he was making his living as an ambulance driver at the time), so he was hugely relieved when two months into the revolution the French army stormed the Commune and killed around twenty-five thousand rebels.

The uprising had been traumatizing for LeBon. And in its aftermath he decided to embark upon an intellectual quest. Could he prove scientifically that mass revolutionary movements were just madness? And, if so, could he dream up ways the elite might benefit from managing the insanity? It could be his ticket into the upper echelons of Parisian society because that was exactly the kind of thing an elite liked to hear.

He began his odyssey by spending a number of years among the Anthropological Society of Paris's huge collection of human skulls. He wanted to demonstrate that aristocrats and businessmen had bigger brains than everybody else and were less likely to succumb to mass hysteria.

"He'd take a skull and fill it with buckshot," Bob Nye explained to me. "Then he'd count the number of pieces of buckshot in order to determine volume."

After measuring 287 skulls, LeBon revealed in an 1879 paper, "Anatomical & Mathematical Researches into the Laws of the Variations of Brain Volume & Their Relation to Intelligence," that the biggest brains did indeed belong to aristocrats and businessmen. He reassured readers who might have been worried that "the body of the Negro is larger than our own" that "their brain is less heavy." Women's brains were less heavy too: "Among the Parisians there are a large number of women whose brains are closer in size to those of gorillas than to the most developed male brains. This inferiority is so obvious that no one can contest it for a moment; only its degree is worth discussion. All psychologists who have studied the intelligence of women, as well as poets and novelists, recognize today that they represent the most inferior forms of human evolution and that they are closer to children and savages than to an adult, civilized man. They excel in fickleness, inconstancy, absence of thought and logic, and incapacity to reason."

He conceded that a few "distinguished women" did exist, but "they are as exceptional as the birth of any monstrosity . . . Consequently, we may neglect them entirely."

And this, he argued, was why feminism must never be allowed to flourish: "A desire to give them the same education, and to propose the same goals for them, is a dangerous chimera. The day when, misunderstanding the inferior occupations which nature has given her, women leave the home and take part in our battles; on this day a social revolution will begin, and everything that maintains the sacred ties of the family will disappear."

"When I was writing my biography of LeBon," Bob Nye told me, "he seemed to me the biggest asshole in the whole of creation."

LeBon's 1879 paper was a disaster. Instead of welcoming him into their ranks, the leading members of the Anthropological Society of Paris mocked him, calling him a misogynist with shoddy scientific methods. "For LeBon, woman is seemingly an accursed being and he predicts abomination and desolation if woman leaves home," the society's secretary-general, Charles Letourneau, announced in a speech. "We naturally have all kinds of reservations about this conclusion."

Stung by the humiliation, LeBon left Paris. He traveled to Arabia. He asked the French Ministry of Public Instruction to fund his trip, proposing to undertake a study of Arabians' racial characteristics, which would be useful were they ever to "fall under French colonial domination," but his request was denied and so he paid for it himself.

Over the next decade, he wrote and self-published several books on the neurological inferiority of Arabians, criminals, and exponents of multiculturalism. He was honing his craft. As Bob Nye solicitously put it in his biography of LeBon, *The Origins of Crowd Psychology*, he was now "concentrating on brevity, using no sources or notes, and writing in a simple and graceful style." What Bob Nye meant was that there were no more skulls and buckshot, no more "evidence" gathering, just certainty. And it was in this style that, in 1895, he published the book that finally made him famous: *The Crowd*.

It begins with LeBon's proud announcement that he isn't part of any recognized scientific society: "To belong to a school is necessarily to espouse its prejudices." And after that, for three hundred pages, he explains why the crowd was insane. "By the mere fact that he forms part of an organized crowd, a man descends several rungs in the ladder of civilization. Isolated, he may be a cultivated individual; in a crowd he is a barbarian—that is, a creature acting by instinct . . . In a crowd every sentiment and act is contagious."

Every simile LeBon uses to describe an individual in a crowd highlights his or her mindlessness. In a crowd we are "microbes" infecting everyone around us, a "grain of sand amid other grains of sand, which the wind stirs up at will." We are impulsive, irritable, irrational: "characteristics which are almost always observed in beings belonging to inferior forms of evolution—in women, savages, and children for instance."

It is no wonder LeBon identified in women, ethnic groups, and children a universal trait of irritability, if that was the way he talked about them.

But *The Crowd* was more than a polemic. Like Jonah Lehrer, LeBon knew that a popular-science book needed a self-improvement message to become successful. And LeBon had two. His first was that we really didn't need to worry ourselves about whether mass revolutionary movements like communism and feminism had a moral reason for existing. They didn't. They were just madness. So it was fine for us to stop worrying about that. And his second message was that a smart orator could, if he knew the tricks, hypnotize the crowd into acquiescence or whip it up to do his bidding. LeBon listed the tricks: "A crowd is only impressed by excessive sentiments. Exaggerate, affirm, resort to repetition, and never attempt to prove anything by reasoning."

The Crowd: A Study of the Popular Mind was, on publication, a runaway success. It was translated into twenty-six languages and gave LeBon what he'd always wanted—a place at the heart of Parisian society, a place he immediately abused in a weird way. He hosted a series of lunches—*les déjeuners du mercredi*—for politicians and prominent society people. He'd sit at the head of the table with a bell by his side. If one of his guests said something he disagreed with, he'd pick up the bell and ring it relentlessly until the person stopped talking.

All over the world, famous people began declaring themselves LeBon fans. Like Mussolini: "I have read all the work of Gustave LeBon and I don't know how many times I have reread *The Crowd*. It is a capital work to which, to this day, I frequently refer." And Goebbels: "Goebbels thinks that no one since the Frenchman LeBon has understood the mind of the masses as well as he," wrote Goebbels's aide Rudolf Semmler in his wartime diary.

Given all of this, you'd think LeBon's work might have at some point stopped being influential. But it never did. I suppose one reason for his enduring success is that we tend to love nothing more than to declare other people insane. And there's another explanation. One psychology experiment more than any other has kept his idea alive. It's the one created in a basement at Stanford University in 1971 by the psychologist Philip Zimbardo.

• • •

Zimbardo was a working-class New York City boy, the son of Sicilian immigrants. After graduating from Brooklyn College in 1954, he taught psychology at Yale and NYU and Columbia before ending up at Stanford in 1971. Crowd theory—or "de-individuation" as it was by then known—preoccupied Zimbardo so deeply that in 1969 he wrote a kind of prose poem to it: "The ageless life force, the cycle of nature, the blood ties, the tribe, the female principle, the irrational, the impulsive, the anonymous chorus, the vengeful furies."

Now, at Stanford, with funding from the U.S. Office of

Naval Research, he set about trying to dramatically prove its existence.

Zimbardo began by placing a small ad in the local paper: "Male college students needed for psychological study of prison life. $15 per day for 1–2 weeks beginning August 14."

After selecting twenty-four applicants, Zimbardo turned the windowless basement of the psychology department into a mock prison, with "cells" and a "solitary confinement room" (a janitor's closet). He split the participants into two groups. Nine would be "prisoners," nine "guards," and the remaining six would be on call. He gave the guards batons and mirrored sunglasses so nobody could see their eyes. He gave himself the role of "superintendent." The prisoners were stripped and put into smocks. Chains were placed on their feet. They were sent to their "cells." And it began.

The experiment was abandoned six days later. It had, as Zimbardo later explained to a congressional hearing, spiraled violently out of control. Zimbardo's fiancée, Christina Maslach, had visited the basement and was horrified by what she saw. The guards were strutting around sadistically, screaming at the prisoners to "fuck the floor" and so on. The prisoners were lying in their cells yelling, "I'm burning up inside, dontchya know? I'm all fucked-up inside!"

Maslach furiously confronted her fiancé: "What are you doing to these boys? You're a stranger to me. The power of the situation has transformed you from the person I thought I knew to this person I don't know."

At this, Zimbardo felt like he'd been slapped awake. She was right. The experiment had turned him evil. "I have to end this," he said to her.

"What we saw was frightening," Zimbardo told the congressional hearing two months later. "In less than a week, human values were suspended and the ugliest, most base, pathological side of human nature surfaced. We were horrified because we saw boys treat other boys as if they were despicable animals, taking pleasure in cruelty."

Zimbardo released a selection of clips from the footage he'd covertly filmed throughout the experiment. In them the guards were seen screaming at the prisoners: "What if I told you to get down on the floor and fuck the floor?" and "You're smiling, [prisoner] 2093, you get down there and do ten push-ups," and "You're Frankenstein. You're Mrs. Frankenstein. Walk like Frankenstein. Hug her. Tell her you love her." And so on. As a result, and to this day, Zimbardo's basement has become for students of social psychology the incarnation of LeBon's crowd—a place of contagion where good people turned evil. As Zimbardo told the BBC in 2002, "We put good people in an evil place and we saw who won."

But I couldn't help thinking that the evil actions captured in Zimbardo's covertly filmed footage looked a bit hammy. Plus, while I knew only too well how a psyche can be mangled by sleep deprivation (I have raised a teething and colicky baby) and by being forced into a windowless room (I once spent an ill-advised week in an inside cabin on the Mediterranean cruise ship MS *Westerdam*, and I'm sure I too would have repeatedly screamed "I'm all fucked-up inside" had it not been for my freedom to visit the Explorations Café and Vista Lounge whenever I liked), at no point, even on the worst nights, did I turn into someone from the Stanford Prison Experiment. What had really gone on in that basement?

. . .

Nowadays John Mark works as a medical coder for the health care company Kaiser Permanente. But for six days back in 1971 he was one of Zimbardo's guards. Tracking down the participants hadn't been an easy task—Zimbardo has never released all of their names—but John Mark has published letters about his memories of the experiment in the Stanford alumni magazine, which was how I discovered him.

"What happens when you tell people you were a guard in the Stanford Prison Experiment?" I asked him over the telephone.

"Everyone assumes I was brutal," he replied. He sighed. "I hear it all the time. You turn on the TV and they'll be talking about anything to do with brutality and they'll drop in 'as was shown in the Stanford Prison Experiment.' They were studying it in my daughter's high school. It really upsets me."

"Why?" I asked.

"It's not *true*," he said. "My days as a guard were pretty

boring. I just sat around. I was on the day shift. I woke the prisoners up, brought them their meals. The vast majority of the time was just hanging out." He paused. "If Zimbardo's conclusion was the true conclusion, wouldn't it have applied to *all* the guards?"

Then he said that if I looked closely at Zimbardo's clips—he wished Zimbardo would release the full footage one day—I'd see that "the only guard who really seemed to lose his mind was Dave Eshelman."

"Dave Eshelman?" I said.

He was right: When you picture the evil guards in Zimbardo's basement, you're really picturing one man—Dave Eshelman. He was the man who yelled "Fuck the floor!" and "You're Frankenstein!" and so on. Social scientists have written papers analyzing Eshelman's every move in there, including the strange detail that the more brutally he behaved, the more American South his accent sounded. I saw at least one analysis of the experiment where the author seemed to find it perfectly plausible that if a person was overcome by a violent madness he'd involuntarily start to sound like someone from Louisiana.

Nowadays Dave Eshelman runs a home-loan company in Saratoga, California. I telephoned him to ask how it felt to personify the evil that lies within all of us.

"I think I did a pretty damn good acting job," he replied.

"What do you mean?" I said.

"This was not a simple case of taking an otherwise normal, well-balanced, rational human being, putting him in a bad situation, and suddenly he turns bad," he said. "I faked it."

He explained. The first night was boring. Everyone was just sitting around. "I thought, *Someone is spending a lot of money to put this thing on and they're not getting any results. So I thought I'd get some action going.*"

He had just seen the Paul Newman prison movie *Cool Hand Luke*, in which a sadistic southern prison warden played by Strother Martin persecutes the inmates. So Dave decided to channel him. His sudden southern accent wasn't some uncontrollable physical transformation—like when Natalie Portman sprouts feathers in *Black Swan*. He was consciously channeling Strother Martin.

"So you faked it to give Zimbardo a better study?" I asked.

"It was completely deliberate on my part," he replied. "I planned it. I mapped it out. I carried it through. It was all done for a purpose. I thought I was doing something good at the time."

After I put the phone down, I wondered if Dave had just told me a remarkable thing—something that might change the way the psychology of evil was taught. He might have just debunked the famous Stanford Prison Experiment. And so I sent a transcript of the interview to the crowd psychologists Steve Reicher and Alex Haslam. They're professors of social psychology—Reicher at St Andrews University and Haslam at the University of Queensland. They've spent their careers studying Zimbardo's work.

They both e-mailed me sounding totally unimpressed by the part I'd thought potentially sensational. "The 'only acting' line is a red herring," Haslam wrote, "because if you are on the receiving end of brutality it doesn't matter if the person was acting or not."

"Acting is not 'unserious,'" Reicher added. "Even if we are performing, the question remains, 'Why did we act in a particular way?'"

But, they both wrote, the conversation with Dave Eshelman was indeed "fascinating and important," as Reicher put it, but for a different reason to the one I'd thought. There was a smoking gun, but it was something I hadn't noticed.

"The really interesting line," Haslam wrote, "is *I thought I was doing something good at the time*. The phrase *doing something good* is quite critical."

Doing something good. This was the opposite of LeBon's and Zimbardo's conclusions. An evil environment hadn't turned Dave evil. Those hundred thousand people who piled on Justine Sacco hadn't been infected with evil. "The irony of those people who use contagion as an explanation," Steve Reicher e-mailed, "is that they saw the TV pictures of the London riots but they didn't go out and riot themselves. It is never true that everyone helplessly joins in with others in a crowd. The riot police don't join in with a rioting crowd. Contagion, it appears, is a problem for others."

Then Reicher told me a story about the only time he ever went to a tennis match. "It was a 'people's day' at Wimbledon, and the hoi polloi were allowed into the show courts. So we were on the number-one court. Three sides were ordinary folk, on the fourth were the members. The game we were watching was fairly boring. So people in the crowd started a Mexican wave. It went round the three 'popular' sides of the court and then the posh folk refused to rise. No contagion there! But the rest of the crowd waited just the time it would have taken for the wave to ripple through the fourth side. Time and again this happened, each time the masses—half jocular—urging the members to rise. And eventually they did in a rather embarrassed way. The ensuing cheer could be heard a long way away. Now, on the surface, perhaps, one might talk of contagion. But actually there is a far more interesting story about the limits of influence coinciding with the boundaries between groups, about class and power . . . Something contagion hides rather than elucidates. Even the most violent crowds are never simply an inchoate explosion. There are always patterns, and those patterns always reflect wider belief systems. So the question we have to ask—which 'contagion' can't answer—is, How come people can come together, often spontaneously, often without leadership, and act together in ideologically intelligible ways? If you can answer that, you get a long way toward understanding human sociality. That is why, instead of being an aberration, crowds are so important and so fascinating."

· · ·

Philip Zimbardo's assistant e-mailed. "Unfortunately he is declining all further interview obligations until midfall due to a full schedule." It was February. I asked her if maybe she could let me know if he was going to be involved in any de-individuation projects. She said she wouldn't. "I receive many many many requests of this sort daily and simply cannot keep up with the requests to remember to be in touch with individuals." I told her I'd spoken to Dave Eshelman and asked if I could at least do a fact check with Dr. Zimbardo. "He may be able to answer a few short questions in mid-May via e-mail," she replied. And so in May I sent her Dave Eshelman's quotes. "Doesn't the phrase 'doing something good' point to the opposite of Dr. Zimbardo's conclusions?" I wrote. "Dave Eshelman hadn't been infected by an evil environment. He was trying to be helpful."

She forwarded my message to Dr. Zimbardo, writing: "Just send back to me! Or I fear he will continue corresponding with you directly!!" (I was accidentally copied in on the exchange.) Zimbardo e-mailed me back later that evening. "Please suspend your naiveté briefly," he wrote. "Eshelman has publicly said he decided to be 'the most cruel, abusive guard imaginable' in videotaped interviews, that the prisoners were his 'puppets,' that he decided to push them as far as he could until they rebelled. They never did and he never let up. In fact, his degrading abuses escalated every night. Trying to be helpful? He created the evil environment that crushed innocent students and prisoners!"

Was Zimbardo right—and was I being naive? Was Dave soft-soaping his brutality all these years later? I did more research and discovered that I wasn't the first person to have found the

Zimbardo experiment a bit contrived. The Boston College psychologist Peter Gray—author of the widely used introductory textbook *Psychology*—published an essay in *Psychology Today* titled "Why Zimbardo's Prison Experiment Isn't in My Textbook."

Twenty-one boys (OK, young men) [there were actually twenty-four] are asked to play a game of prisoners and guards. It's 1971. There have recently been many news reports about prison riots and the brutality of guards. So, in this game, what are these young men supposed to do? Are they supposed to sit around talking pleasantly with one another about girlfriends, movies, and such? No, of course not. This is a study of prisoners and guards, so their job clearly is to act like prisoners and guards—or, more accurately, to act out their stereotyped views of what prisoners and guards do. Surely, Professor Zimbardo, who is right there watching them (as the Prison Superintendent) would be disappointed if, instead, they had just sat around chatting pleasantly and having tea. Much research has shown that participants in psychological experiments are highly motivated to do what they believe the researchers want them to do.

Gray felt Zimbardo's critical error was in awarding himself the role of superintendent, instead of being some remote observer. And he was no aloof superintendent. Before the experiment began, he gave his guards a pep talk, as he later recounted in his own book *The Lucifer Effect*.

"We cannot physically abuse or torture them," I said. "We can create boredom. We can create a sense of frustration. We can create fear in them, to some degree. We can create a notion of the arbitrariness that governs their lives, which are totally controlled by us, by the system, by you, me, [Warden] Jaffe. They'll have no privacy at all, there will be constant surveillance—nothing they do will go unobserved. They will have no freedom of action. They will be able to do nothing and say nothing that we don't permit. We're going to take away their individuality in various ways. They're going to be wearing uniforms, and at no time will anybody call them by name; they will have numbers and be called only by their numbers. In general, what all this should create in them is a sense of powerlessness. We have total power in the situation. They have none."

. . .

For Gustave LeBon, a crowd was just a great ideology-free explosion of madness—a single blob of violent color without variation. But that wasn't Twitter. Twitter did not speak with one voice. Within Justine Sacco's pile-on, there had been misogynists: "Somebody (HIV+) must rape this bitch and we'll see if her skin color protects her from AIDS." There had been humanitarians: "If @JustineSacco's unfortunate words about AIDS bother you, join me in supporting @CARE's work in Africa." There had been corporations promoting products, like the airplane Wi-Fi provider Gogo: "Next time you plan to tweet something stupid before you take off, make sure you are getting on a @Gogo flight! CC: @JustineSacco."

All these people had, just as Steve Reicher said, come together spontaneously, without leadership. I wasn't one of them. But I'd piled on plenty of people like Justine. I'd been beguiled by the new technology—a toddler crawling toward a gun. Just like with Dave Eshelman, it was the desire to do something good that had propelled me. Which was definitely a better thing to be propelled by than group madness. But my desire had taken a lot of scalps—I'd torn apart a *lot* of people I couldn't now remember—which made me suspect that it was coming from some very weird dark well, some place I really didn't want to think about. Which was why I had to think about it.

Six

Doing Something Good

I am a nobody," said Hank, "just a guy with a family and a job, a middle America–type guy."

Hank wasn't his real name. He'd managed to keep that aspect of himself a secret. He was talking to me via Google Hangouts from his kitchen in a suburban house in a West Coast American town I promised him I wouldn't name. He looked frail, fidgety, the sort of man more comfortable working alone at a computer than talking to a human stranger via one.

On March 18, 2013, Hank was in the audience at a conference for tech developers in Santa Clara, California, when a stupid joke popped into his head, which he murmured to his friend Alex.

"What was the joke?" I asked him.

"It was so bad I don't remember the exact words," he said. "It was about a fictitious piece of hardware that has a really big dongle—a ridiculous dongle. We were giggling about that. It wasn't even conversation-level volume."

A few moments earlier, Hank and Alex had been giggling over some other Beavis-and-Butt-head-type tech in-joke about "forking someone's repo." "We'd decided it was a new form of flattery," Hank explained. "A guy had been onstage presenting his new project and Alex said, 'I would fork that guy's repo.'"

(In tech jargon "to fork" means to take a copy of another person's software so you can work on it independently. Another word for software is "repository." This is why "forking someone's repo" works both as a term of flattery and also as sexual innuendo—just in case you wanted to know. I think it is a very special sort of hell where you're compelled to explain to a journalist some terrible throwaway joke you made ten months earlier and the journalist keeps saying, "I'm sorry. I still don't get it," but that was the hell Hank found himself in during his Google Hangouts chat with me.)

Moments after making the dongle joke, Hank half noticed the woman sitting in front of them at the conference stand up, turn around, and take a photograph. Hank thought she was taking a picture of the crowd. So he looked forward, trying not to mess up her shot.

It's a little painful to look at this photograph now— knowing what was about to happen to them. Those mischie-

Hank is on the left, Alex on the right.

vous, stupid smiles that follow in the wake of a dongle joke successfully shared would be Hank's and Alex's last smiles for a while.

Ten minutes after the photograph was taken, a conference organizer came down the aisle and said to Hank and Alex, "Can you come with me?"

They were taken into an office and told there'd been a complaint about sexual comments. "I immediately apologized," Hank said. "I knew exactly what they were talking about. I told them what we'd said, and that we didn't mean for it to come across as a sexual comment, and that we were sorry if someone overheard and was offended. They were like, 'Okay. I see what happened.'"

And that was that. The incident passed. Hank and Alex

were badly shaken up—"We're nerdy guys and confrontation isn't something we handle well. It's not something we're accustomed to"—and so they decided to leave the conference early.

They were on their way to the airport when they started wondering exactly *how* the woman sitting in front of them had conveyed her complaint to the conference organizers. They suddenly felt anxious about this. The nightmarish possibility was that it had been communicated in the form of a public tweet. And so, with apprehension, they had a look.

Adria Richards
@adriarichards
Follow

Not cool. Jokes about forking repo's in a sexual way and "big" dongles. Right behind me #pycon
pic.twitter.com/Hv1bkeOsYP
10:32 PM - 17 Mar 13

26 RETWEETS 17 FAVORITES

A bolt of anxiety shot through Hank. He quickly scanned her replies, but there was nothing much—just the odd congratulation from a few of her 9,209 followers for the "noble" way she'd "educated" the men behind her. He noticed ruefully that a few days earlier the woman—her name was Adria Richards—had herself tweeted a stupid penis joke. She'd suggested to a friend that he put socks down his pants to bewilder TSA agents at the airport. Hank relaxed a little.

The next day Adria Richards followed up her tweet with a blog post:

> Yesterday, I publicly called out a group of guys at the PyCon conference who were not being respectful to the community.

She explained the background—how she was a "developer evangelist at a successful start-up" and that while the men had been giggling about big dongles, the presenter onstage was talking about initiatives to bring more women into the industry. In fact, he'd just projected onto the screen a photograph of a little girl at a tech workshop.

> Accountability was important. These guys sitting right behind me felt safe in the crowd. I got that and realized that being anonymous was fueling their behavior. This is known as Deindividuation. Theories of deindividuation propose [here Adria was quoting from Wikipedia] that it is a psychological state of decreased self-evaluation and decreased evaluation apprehension causing antinormative and disinhibited behavior. Deindividuation theory

seeks to provide an explanation for a variety of antinor-mative collective behavior, such as violent crowds, lynch mobs, etc.

Deindividuation. Here was Gustave LeBon and Philip Zimbardo springing into life once again, this time within Adria's blog.

I stood up slowly, turned around and took three, clear photos . . . There is something about crushing a little kid's dream that gets me really angry . . .

It takes three words to make a difference:

"That's not cool." . . .

Yesterday the future of programming was on the line and I made myself heard.

—ADRIA RICHARDS, *But You're a Girl* BLOG,
MARCH 18, 2013

But Hank had already been called into his boss's office and fired.

• • •

I packed up all my stuff in a box," Hank said, "then I went outside to call my wife. I'm not one to shed tears but . . . When I got in the car with my wife I just . . . I've got three kids. Getting fired was terrifying."

That night Hank made his only public statement. (Like

Justine and Jonah, he had never spoken to a journalist about what had happened until he spoke to me.) He posted a short message on the discussion board Hacker News.

> Hi, I'm the guy who made a comment about big dongles. First of all I'd like to say I'm sorry. I really did not mean to offend anyone and I really do regret the comment and how it made Adria feel. She had every right to report me to staff, and I defend her position . . . [But] as a result of the picture she took I was let go from my job today. Which sucks because I have 3 kids and I really liked that job.
>
> She gave me no warning, she smiled while she snapped the pic and sealed my fate.

"The next day," Hank said, "Adria Richards called my company asking them to ask me to remove the portion of my apology that stated I lost my job as a result of her tweet."

•   •   •

I sent Adria an interview request. "All right, pitch me via e-mail and if relevant, I'll respond," she replied. So I pitched. Successfully. We agreed to meet two weeks later. "We will meet in a public place for safety reasons," Adria wrote. "Make sure to bring along your ID for verification."

We settled on the international check-in desks at San Francisco Airport. I was expecting someone fiercer. But when I saw her half wave at me from across the terminal, she didn't seem fierce at all. She seemed introverted and delicate, just like how Hank had come across over Google Hangouts. We found a café and she told me about the moment it all began for her—the moment she overheard the comment about the big dongle.

"Have you ever had an altercation at school and you could feel the hairs rise up on your back?" she asked me.

"You felt fear?" I asked.

"Danger," she said. "Clearly my body was telling me, 'You are unsafe.'"

Which was why, she said, she "slowly stood up, rotated from my hips, and took three photos." She tweeted one, "with a very brief summary of what they said. Then I sent another tweet describing my location. Right? And then the third tweet was the [conference's] code of conduct."

"Danger?" I said. "What were you imagining might . . . ?"

"Have you ever heard that thing, 'Men are afraid that women will laugh at them and women are afraid that men will kill them'?" she said.

I told Adria that people might consider that an overblown thing to say. She had, after all, been in the middle of a tech conference with eight hundred bystanders.

"Sure," Adria replied. "And those people would probably be white and they would probably be male."

This seemed a weak gambit. Men can sometimes be correct. There is some Latin for this kind of logical fallacy. It's called an ad hominem attack. When someone can't defend a criticism against them, they change the subject by attacking the criticizer.

"Somebody getting fired is pretty bad," I said. "I know

you didn't *call* for him to be fired. But you must have felt pretty bad."

"Not too bad," she said. She thought more and shook her head decisively. "He's a white male. I'm a black Jewish female. He was saying things that could be inferred as offensive to me, sitting in front of him. I do have empathy for him but it only goes so far. If he had Down syndrome and he accidentally pushed someone off a subway that would be different.... I've seen things where people are like, 'Adria didn't know what she was doing by tweeting it.' Yes I did."

• • •

The evening Hank posted his statement on Hacker News, outsiders began to involve themselves in his and Adria's story. Hank started receiving messages of support from men's-rights bloggers. He didn't respond to any of them. Later a Gucci Little Piggy blogger wrote that Hank's Hacker News message had revealed him to be a man with

a complete lack of backbone . . . by apologizing you are just saying, "I am a weak enemy—do with me what you will." [In publicly shaming Hank, Adria had] complete and utter power over his children. That doesn't piss this guy off?

At the same time that Hank was being feted and then insulted by the men's-rights bloggers, Adria discovered she was getting discussed on a famous meeting place for trolls: 4chan/b/.

A father of three is out of a job because a silly joke he was telling a friend was overheard by someone with more power than sense. Let's crucify this cunt.

Kill her.

Cut out her uterus with an xacto knife.

Someone sent Adria a photograph of a beheaded woman with tape over her mouth. Adria's face was superimposed onto the bodies of porn actors. Websites were created to teach people how to make the superimposing look seamless, by matching skin tones. On Facebook someone wrote, "I hope I can find Adria, kidnap her, put a torture bag over her head, and shoot a .22 subsonic round right into her fucking skull. Fuck that bitch make her pay make her obey." (That message, Adria told me, although I couldn't confirm it, was from a student at the New York City College of Technology.)

"Death threats and rape threats only feed her cause," someone eventually wrote on 4chan/b/. "I don't mean stop doing things. Just think first. Do something productive."

Then her employer's website and servers came under a massive DDoS attack, which caused them to crash—the automated version of one person or even thousands sitting at a computer manually pressing refresh relentlessly until the targeted website becomes overpowered and collapses. A group of attackers said the attacks would stop if Adria was fired. Hours later she was fired—publicly and without warning, according to SendGrid's CEO, for dividing the community she was supposed to unite.

"I slept on couches for most of 2013," she later emailed me. "I cried a lot during this time, journaled, and escaped by watching Netflix. How do I feel about losing my job? I didn't expect it. SendGrid [her employers] threw me under the bus. I felt betrayed. I felt abandoned. I felt ashamed. I felt rejected. I felt alone."

. . .

A few days before I flew to San Francisco to meet Adria, I posted a message on 4chan/b/ asking for anyone personally involved in her destruction to contact me. The message was deleted in less than a minute. I posted another request. That one vanished after a few seconds. Somebody inside 4chan was silently erasing me whenever I tried to make contact. But my messages happened to coincide with the arrests of some hard-core 4chan trolls and DDoSers and activists, so suddenly there were real names out there. Which was how I came to meet a twenty-one-year-old 4chan denizen, Mercedes Haefer.

In her Facebook photograph Mercedes wears a comedy mustache and bunny ears. Now we sat opposite each other in a vast, opulent loft apartment above an old grocery store on the Lower East Side of Manhattan. It belongs to her lawyer, Stanley Cohen. He's spent his career representing anarchists and communists and squatter groups and Hamas, and now he was representing Mercedes.

The crime she was accused of (and would later plead guilty

to; she is awaiting sentencing as I write this) is that in November 2010 she and thirteen other 4chan users DDoS'd
PayPal as revenge for their refusing to accept donations to
WikiLeaks. You could donate to the Ku Klux Klan via PayPal
but not to WikiLeaks.

The FBI showed up at her Las Vegas apartment one day at
six a.m. "I answered the door and they said, 'Mercedes, do
you mind putting your pants on?' To be honest, being arrested is really fun. You get to troll the FBI, you get to wear
fancy handcuffs, you get to pick the music in the car. But the
indictment was boring. I napped through it."

I spent a few hours with Mercedes. She was, on the surface, quite troll-like—a lover of jubilant online chaos. She
told me about her favorite 4chan thread. It was started by "a
guy who's genuinely in love with his dog, and his dog went in
heat, and so he went around collecting samples and inject-
ing them into his penis and he fucked his dog and got her
pregnant and they're his puppies." Mercedes laughed. "That's
the thread I told the FBI about when they asked me about
4chan, and some of the officers actually got up and left
the room."

This aspect of Mercedes wasn't so interesting to me because I didn't see this story as being a story about trolls.
Focusing on trolls would be taking the easy option—blaming
the renaissance of public shaming on some ludicrous, outrageous minority. A scattering of trolls may have piled on Justine and Adria, but trolls didn't fell those people. People like
me felled them.

But I got to know and like Mercedes during the months

that followed—we e-mailed each other a lot—and she really wasn't much of a troll at all. Her motives were kinder than that. She was also someone whose shaming frenzy was motivated by the desire to do good. She told me about the time 4chan tracked down a boy who had been posting videos of himself on YouTube physically abusing his cat "and daring people to stop him." 4chan users found him "and let the entire town know he was a sociopath. Ha ha! And the cat was taken away from him and adopted."

(Of course, the boy might have been a sociopath. But Mercedes and the other 4chan people had no evidence of that—no idea what may or may not have been happening in his home life to turn him that way.)

I asked Mercedes what sorts of people gathered on 4chan.

"A lot of them are bored, understimulated, overpersecuted, powerless kids," she replied. "They know they can't be anything they want. So they went to the Internet. On the Internet we have power in situations where we would otherwise be powerless."

This was a period of sustained draconian prosecutorial bombardment—an effort by authorities to subdue people like Mercedes into submission. But when I asked her if she thought the prosecutions would end their DDoSing and trolling campaigns, her response was sharp and trenchant.

"The police are trying to claim the area," she said. By "area," she meant the Internet. "Just like in the cities. They gentrify the downtown, move all the poor people into ghettos, and then start trolling the ghettos, stopping and frisking everyone."

As it happened, shortly before I met Mercedes, the New York Police Department released figures on how many times their officers had stopped and frisked New Yorkers during the previous year. It was 684,330 times. That was 1,800 stop and frisks each day. Of those 1,800 people—according to the New York Civil Liberties Union—nearly nine out of ten "have been completely innocent."

In July 2012 a civil rights lawyer with the Center for Constitutional Rights, Nahal Zamani, interviewed victims of the policy for a research paper, "Stop and Frisk: The Human Impact."

> Several interviewees said that being stopped and frisked makes you "feel degraded and humiliated." One went on to say: "When they stop you in the street, and then everybody's looking . . . it does degrade you. And then people get the wrong perception of you. That kind of colors people's thoughts toward you, [people] might start thinking that you're into some illegal activity, when you're not. Just because the police [are] just stopping you for—just randomly. That's humiliating [on] its own." . . . [Another said,] "It made me feel violated, humiliated, harassed, shameful, and of course very scared."

By some strange circular coincidence, it was Jonah Lehrer's fellow *New Yorker* writer Malcolm Gladwell who had popularized the stop-and-frisk policy. When it was first implemented in the 1990s—it was known as broken-windows policing back then—Gladwell wrote a landmark *New Yorker* essay about it, "The Tipping Point." He called it "miraculous." There was a correlation between coming down heavy on petty criminals like graffiti artists and fare dodgers, his essay argued, and New York's sudden decline in murders.

"A strange and unprecedented transformation" was happening across New York City, Gladwell observed. There used to be volleys of gunfire. Now there were "ordinary people on the streets at dusk, small children riding their bicycles, old people on benches, people coming out of the subways alone. Sometimes the most modest of changes can bring about enormous effects."

Gladwell's essay was a sensation—one of the most influential articles in the magazine's history. It sold the aggressive policing tactic to thoughtful, liberal New York City people— the sort of people who wouldn't normally support such a draconian idea. He gave a generation of liberals permission to be more conservative. He became a marketing tool for broken-windows policing. His book *The Tipping Point* went on to sell two million copies, launching his career and the careers of the countless other pop-science writers who followed in his footsteps—like Jonah Lehrer.

But Gladwell's essay was wrong. Subsequent data revealed that violent crime had been dropping in New York City for five years before broken-windows policing was implemented. It was plummeting at the same rate all over America. This included places—like Chicago and Washington, D.C.—where war hadn't been declared on fare dodgers and graffiti artists. When I interviewed Gladwell in 2013 for a separate project—BBC's *The Culture Show*—I brought up the topic of stop and frisk and broken-windows policing with him. A pained, remorseful look crossed his face. "I was too in love with the broken-windows notion," he said. "I was so enamored by the metaphorical simplicity of that idea that I overstated its importance."

Stop and frisk continued through the 2000s and into the 2010s, and one by-product of it was that some repeatedly frisked young people sought revenge in online activism—by joining 4chan. It wasn't only Mercedes who told me this. Soon after we met, I had a cloak-and-dagger meeting outside a subway station in Queens with a 4chan friend of hers. A battered car pulled up. The driver was young, white, of Spanish heritage, and wore a big crucifix. I still don't know his real name. He said I should call him by his Internet name: Troy.

He took me to a café where he grumbled about how things weren't like they used to be, about the good old days when you couldn't leave your mobile phone on a café table around here without its being stolen. I told Troy that the good old days sounded terrible to me, but he explained that with gentrification comes collateral damage—constant stop and frisks of any young person who doesn't look like a preppy hipster: "Going to the store, coming home from school, ruining your whole day. It's disgusting. It's dangerous to walk the borders around here." It was these police inequities that compelled Troy to join 4chan, he told me.

"The police are saying, 'Look at what we can do to you on your own turf,'" Mercedes continued. "'This is not your space. It's our space, and we're letting you exist here.' People socialize on Facebook because where do you go to loiter in New York anymore? The Internet is our space and they're trying to take it, and it's not going to happen because it's the Internet."

"And you know more about how it works than they do?" I asked her.

"Fuck them," she said. "They're idiots. If you understood medicine in Massachusetts at a certain time, you were a witch and they would burn you. There aren't a lot of people these days who can get past Facebook. So explain to them how a router works and you're a magician. You're a dark wizard. Then they say, 'We need to lock them away forever because we don't understand how else to stop them.' Part of the reason all these kids have become experts on the Internet is because they don't have power anywhere else. Skilled trade is shrinking. That's why they went there. And then, holy shit, it blew up."

I asked Mercedes about the attack on Justine. She said, "Sacco? The one that got those guys fired for joking about dongles?"

"That was Adria Richards," I said. "Justine Sacco was the AIDS-tweet woman."

"Well, that was Twitter," she said. "Twitter is a different beast from 4chan. It has more regular morals and values than 4chan. Adria Richards got attacked because she got a guy fired for making a dongle joke that wasn't directed at anyone. He wasn't hurting anyone. She was impeding his freedom of speech and the Internet spanked her for it."

"And Justine Sacco?" I said.

"There's a fair understanding on the Internet of what it means to be the little guy," Mercedes said, "the guy rich white

assholes make jokes about. And so the issue with Justine
Sacco is that she's a rich white person who made a joke about
black sick people who will die soon. So for a few hours, Justine Sacco got to find out what it feels like to be the little guy
everyone makes fun of. Dragging down Justine Sacco felt like
dragging down every rich white person who's ever gotten
away with making a racist joke because they could. She
thought her black AIDS joke was funny because she doesn't
know what it's like to be a disadvantaged black person or be
diagnosed with AIDS." She paused. "Some sorts of crimes
can only be handled by public consensus and shaming. It's a
different kind of court. A different kind of jury."

I asked Mercedes to explain to me one of the great mysteries
of modern shamings—why they were so breathtakingly mi-
sogynistic. Nobody had used the language of sexual violence
against Jonah, but when Justine and Adria stepped out of
line, the rape threats were instant. And the 4chan people
were about the most unpleasant.

"Yeah, it's a bit extreme," Mercedes replied. "4chan takes
the worst thing it can imagine that person going through and
shouts for that to happen. I don't think it was a threat that
anyone intended to carry through. And I think a lot of its use
really did mean 'destroy' rather than 'sexually assault.'" She
paused. "But 4chan aims to degrade the target, right? And
one of the highest degradations for women in our culture is
rape. We don't talk about rape of men, so I think it doesn't
occur to most people as a male degradation. With men, they
talk about getting them fired. In our society men are sup-

posed to be employed. If they're fired, they lose masculinity points. With Donglegate she pointlessly robbed that man of his employment. She degraded his masculinity. And so the community responded by degrading her femininity."

. . .

The death threats and rape threats against Adria continued even after she was fired. "Things got very bad for her," Hank told me. "She had to disappear for six months. Her entire life was being evaluated by the Internet. It was not a good situation for her at all."

"Have you ever met her?" I asked him.

"No," Hank replied. "There's never been any contact between us since she turned around and took my photograph."

Ten months had passed since that day. Hank had had ten months to allow his feelings about her to settle into something coherent, so I asked him what he thought of her now.

"I think that nobody deserves what she went through," he replied.

. . .

Maybe it was [Hank] who started all of this," Adria told me in the café at the San Francisco airport. "No one would have known he got fired until he complained," she said. "Maybe he's to blame for complaining that he got fired. Maybe he secretly seeded the hate groups. Right?"

I was so taken aback by this suggestion that I didn't say

anything in defense of Hank at the time. But later I felt bad that I hadn't stuck up for him. So I e-mailed her. I told her what he had told me—how he'd refused to engage with any of the bloggers or trolls who sent him messages of support. I added that I felt Hank was within his rights to post the message on Hacker News revealing he'd been fired.

Adria replied that she was happy to hear that Hank "wasn't active in driving their interests to mount the raid attack," but she held him responsible for it anyway. It was "his own actions that resulted in his own firing, yet he framed it in a way to blame me . . . If I had a spouse and two kids to support I certainly would not be telling 'jokes' like he was doing at a conference. Oh but wait, I have compassion, empathy, morals and ethics to guide my daily life choices. I often wonder how people like Hank make it through life seemingly unaware of how 'the other' lives in the same world he does but with countless less opportunities."

●　●　●

I asked Hank if he found himself behaving differently since the incident. Had it altered how he lived his life?

"I distance myself from female developers a little bit now," Hank replied. "I'm not as friendly. There's humor, but it's very mundane. You just don't know. I can't afford another Donglegate."

"Give me an example," I said. "So you're in your new workplace"—Hank was offered another job right away—"and you're talking to a female developer. In what way do you act differently toward her?"

"Well," Hank said. "We don't have any female developers at the place I'm working at now. So."

Another picture Adria took at the tech conference
on the day of the dongle joke.

 • • •

Y ou've got a new job now, right?" I said to Adria.
  "No," she said.

 • • •

A dria's father was an alcoholic. He used to beat Adria's mother. He hit her with a hammer. He knocked all her teeth out. After he left them, Adria's mother fell apart. She didn't feed or wash Adria. "Going to school was hard," Adria wrote on her blog in February 2013. "The kids would tease me because my clothes were dirty and my shoes had holes.

My hair was a complete mess. I felt ashamed. I was hungry all the time." Adria ended up in foster care.

She sent me a letter she'd written to her father. "It's Adria! How are you doing? I know it's been a very, very long time. I want to see you. I love you, daddy. I'm 26 years old now. If you get this, please contact me as I really would love to see you."

Her father didn't write back. She hasn't heard from him in decades. She thinks he's probably dead.

When I asked Adria if her childhood trauma might have influenced the way she'd regarded Hank and Alex, she said no. "They say the same thing for rape victims. If you've been raped, you think all men are rapists." She paused. "No. These dudes were straight up being not cool."

• • •

I had shamed a lot of people. A lot of people had revealed their true selves for a moment and I had shrewdly noticed their masks slipping and quick-wittedly alerted others. But I couldn't remember any of them now. So many forgotten outrages. Although I did remember one. The deviant was the *Sunday Times* and *Vanity Fair* columnist A. A. Gill. His wrongdoing was a column he wrote about shooting a baboon on safari in Tanzania: "I'm told they can be tricky to shoot. They run up trees, hang on for grim life. They die hard, baboons. But not this one. A soft-nosed .357 blew his lungs out." A. A. Gill's motive? "I wanted to get a sense of what it might be like to kill someone, a stranger."

I'd been about the first person to alert social media.

This is because A. A. Gill always gives my television documentaries very bad reviews, so I tend to keep a vigilant eye on things he can be got for. And within minutes it was everywhere.

> Following in Jan Moir's footsteps, "AA Gill" is now a trending topic on Twitter, where [he is] being denounced for the murder of a primate. The Guardian, of course, is fanning the flames. They've been in touch with Steve Taylor, a spokesman for the League Against Cruel Sports, who said: "This is morally completely indefensible. If he wants to know what it [is] like to shoot a human, he should take aim at his own leg."
>
> —Will Heaven, *The Daily Telegraph*,
> October 27, 2009

Amid the hundreds of congratulatory messages I received, one stuck out: "Were you a bully at school?"

Was I a *bully* at school?

When my son was five years old, he one day asked me, "Did you used to be fat?"

"Yes," I said. "I was fat when I was sixteen. And I was thrown in a lake for being fat."

"Wow!" Joel said.

"There are two lessons to be learned from this," I said. "Don't be a bully and don't be fat."

"Will you show me what it looked like?" he asked me.

"Me being fat or me being thrown in a lake?" I asked.

"Both," he said.

I puffed up my cheeks, waddled self-consciously around the room, fell over, and said, "Splash!"

"Will you do it again in slow motion?" said Joel. "And put a cushion under your shirt?"

So I did. This time I added dialogue: "Please don't throw me in the lake! No! Splash!"

"Will you sound more scared?" said Joel.

"PLEASE!" I shouted. "I might drown. Please. No, NO!"

Joel glanced, startled, at me. It was his fault that I'd gone that far. He'd been like Sam Peckinpah, forever directing me to make it more grotesque, basically getting me to mime the swallowing of dirty water as I struggled to the surface. But I think he'd trusted that within my reenactment I would at all times retain some dignity.

But then he smiled.

"You were SO fat!" he said.

My life has basically been a good one, but my mind forever returns to those two years in Cardiff—between 1983 and 1985—when I was bullied every day, stripped and blindfolded, and thrown across the playground. Those years hover over me when I walk into new rooms, meet new people.

* * *

It seemed to me that all the people involved in the Hank and Adria story thought they were doing something good. But they only revealed that our imagination is so limited, our arsenal of potential responses so narrow, that the only thing anyone can think to do with an inappropriate shamer like Adria is to punish her with a shaming. All of the shamers had themselves come from a place of shame, and it really felt parochial and self-defeating to instinctively slap shame onto shame like a clumsy builder covering cracks.

I remembered something that Jonah Lehrer had said to me back in Runyon Canyon. He'd said, "I look forward to reading your book so I can learn how people find a way out of shame."

I hadn't thought about writing some sort of a public-shaming recovery guide. But what he'd said stayed with me. Were there old-timer shamees out there who had managed to survive theirs intact and who could offer enlightenment to the distraught victims of this new shame dynamic? Were there people out there who had found a way out of shame? I knew just where to start.

Seven

Journey to a Shame-Free Paradise

**F1 BOSS MAX MOSLEY HAS SICK NAZI ORGY
WITH 5 HOOKERS
EXCLUSIVE: SON OF FASCIST HITLER LOVER
IN SEX SHAME**

Formula One motor racing chief Max Mosley is today exposed as a secret sadomasochist sex pervert. The son of infamous British wartime fascist leader Oswald Mosley is filmed romping with five hookers at a depraved NAZI-STYLE orgy in a torture dungeon.

Before hammering away at the girls he plays a cowering death camp inmate himself, having his GENITALS inspected and his hair searched for LICE—mocking the humiliating way Jews were treated by SS death camp guards in World War II . . .

At one point the wrinkled 67-year-old yells "she needs more of ze punishment!" while brandishing a LEATHER STRAP over a brunette's naked bottom. Then the lashes rain down as Mosley counts them out in German: "Eins! Zwei! Drei! Vier! Fünf! Sechs!"

With each blow, the girl yelps in pain as grinning, gray-haired Mosley becomes clearly aroused. And after the beating, he makes her perform a sex act on him.

His Jew-hating father—who had Hitler as guest of honor at his marriage—would have been proud of his warped son's command of German as he struts around looking for bottoms to whack. Our investigators obtained a graphic video of his sick antics.

—NEVILLE THURLBECK, *News of the World*,
MARCH 30, 2008

Max Mosley sat across from me in the living room of his West London mews house. We were alone. His wife, Jean, was at their other house, where she now spends most of her time. As Max told the *Financial Times*'s Lucy Kellaway in 2011, "She doesn't like going out, she doesn't want to meet people."

Nobody I could think of had ridden out a public shaming

as immaculately as Max Mosley had. A powerful and hitherto not especially well-liked society man and the head of the
FIA, Formula One racing's governing body, had been photo-
graphed by the *News of the World*'s hidden cameras in the
most startling sex situation imaginable, especially given his
particular Nazi associations, and he had somehow managed
to emerge from the scandal completely intact. In fact, it was
even better than intact. People liked him more than ever.
Some people thought of him as a standard-bearer for our
right to feel unashamed. That's how I thought of him. And
now Max was every shamee's aspiration. I wanted him to talk
me through how he did it.

But he looked embarrassed by my question. "I'm no good
at introspection," he said.

"But you must have some clue," I said. "You stood at the
newsstand that Sunday morning reading the *News of the
World* article . . ."

"It was immediate," Max said. "It was a *whoosh*. It was,
'This is war.'" Then he trailed off and gave me a look to say,
I'm sorry, but I really don't do introspection.

I think he was as curious about the mystery as I was. But
he didn't know the answer.

"You had a strange childhood . . ." I tried.

"I suppose my upbringing toughened me up a bit," he said.
"From a very early age, I realized that my parents weren't like
other people's parents . . ."

Until that "Sick Nazi Orgy" headline, the thing Max Mosley
was most famous for—unless you were a Formula One racing

fan—was his parents. Max's father was Sir Oswald Mosley, the founder in 1932 of the British Union of Fascists. He gave Nuremberg-style speeches in London during which hecklers were illuminated by spotlights and viciously beaten in front of the crowd. Oswald Mosley stood onstage and watched. Max's mother was the beautiful socialite Diana Mitford. She and her sister Unity were so besotted by Hitler—with whom they both became friendly—they'd send each other letters like this one, from Unity to Diana:

23rd December 1935

> *The Führer was heavenly, in his best mood and very gay. There was a choice of two soups and he tossed a coin to see which one he would have, and he was so sweet doing it. He asked after you and I told him you were coming soon. He talked a lot about Jews, which was lovely.*
>
> > *With best love and Heil Hitler,*
> > *Bobo.*

Hitler attended Oswald Mosley and Diana Mitford's wedding, which took place at Joseph Goebbels's house in 1936. Max was born in 1940, and when he was a few months old, his parents were interred for the duration of the war at Holloway Prison in North London. Those were his first memories—visiting his imprisoned parents, "which doesn't strike you as unusual when you're three, but as you get older, you realize they're disliked by a big section of society. Still, they were my parents, so I was completely on their side. When someone argued with me about my father, it was easy for me to win because I knew all the facts."

"What did people say about your father that wasn't true?" I asked.

"Oh, you know, 'He was a friend of Hitler.' Well, without going into whether that was a good or a bad thing, I knew he only met Hitler twice and he actually didn't like him. My mother was a friend, undoubtedly, and her sister, but not my father."

"Why didn't your father like Hitler?" I asked.

"I think he thought he was . . ." Max screwed up his face.

"A bit blah?" I said.

"Something of a poseur," agreed Max. "To that sort of Englishman. But then again, he quite got on with Mussolini, of whom the same could have been said. I suspect he saw Hitler as this other man who was in the same line of business as him but much more successful. And my mother liked him. I don't think there was any affair but . . . well, you can see it. Anyway. To me the whole thing has been an enormous nuisance and encumbrance."

Max drifted into the motor-racing world. Nobody cared about his father there. As he told *Autosport* magazine in 2000, he knew he was where he belonged when he overheard someone say, "Mosley. He must be some relation of Alf Moseley, the coachbuilder." Max was in his mid-twenties when he started in the racing world, and he had just begun going to S&M clubs.

"Are S&M clubs comfortable places to be?" I asked him. "Are they relaxing?"

"Well, yes," Max said. From his look, I guessed he considered them places of integrity—nonexploitative, shame-free retreats from a world that overvalues shame as a weapon.

"Were you worried about getting caught?" I asked.

"I was careful," he said. "Especially when I began seriously annoying a big section of the car industry." What Max meant was that by the early 1990s he had become a campaigner to reform car-safety laws, forcing manufacturers to carry out crash tests. "And when you think of what they did to Ralph Nader . . ."

· · ·

Ralph Nader. In 1961 a young man named Frederick Condon crashed his car. Back then, sharp edges and no seat belts were considered stylish in car interiors. But the sharp edges turned Frederick Condon into a paraplegic. And so a friend of his—the lawyer Ralph Nader—began lobbying for mandatory seat-belt laws. Which was why General Motors hired prostitutes to follow Nader into stores—a Safeway supermarket and a pharmacy—to seduce and then blackmail him.

"It happened twice," Nader told me, when I telephoned him. "They were women in their mid-to-late twenties. They were pretty good. They both acted in a very spontaneous manner, not a furtive manner. They started a little small talk. Then they got down to it."

"What did they say to you?" I asked him.

"The first woman said, 'Would you help me move some furniture in my apartment?' And the other one said, 'We're having a discussion on foreign affairs. Would you like to join it?' Here I was, at the cookie counter!" Nader laughed. "'Foreign affairs'!" he said.

"And all because you wanted them to put seat belts in cars?" I said.

"They didn't want the government to tell them how to build their cars," he replied. "They were very libertarian that way, to put it mildly. They had private detectives follow me everywhere. They spent ten thousand dollars just to find out if I had a driver's license. If I didn't have a driver's license, they could have called me un-American, you see?"

Eventually, General Motors was forced to admit the plot and apologize to Nader in a congressional hearing. The incident proved to him, and later to Max, that the car industry was not above trying to shame its opponents into silence in its battle against safety do-gooders, and that people in high places were prepared to ingeniously deploy shaming as a means of moneymaking and social control. Maybe we only notice it happening when it's done too audaciously or poorly, as it had been with Ralph Nader.

• • •

One Sunday morning in the spring of 2008, a PR man telephoned Max to ask him if he'd seen the *News of the World*. "He said, 'There's a big story about you.' So I went to the newsstand."

And as Max stared at the grainy photographs that millions of Britons were simultaneously staring at—a naked Max being bent over and spanked by women in German uniform—a line from *Othello* came into his head: *"I have lost my reputation! I have lost the immortal part of myself and what remains is bestial."*

All he'd worked for had been pushed away by a thing he had always considered a tiny part of his life. He took the newspaper home and showed it to his wife. She thought he'd had it specially printed as a joke. And then she realized that it wasn't a joke.

Max's behavior from that moment on was the opposite of Jonah's. He gave an interview to BBC Radio 4 in which he said that, yes, his sex life was strange, but when it comes to sex, people think and say and do strange things, and only an idiot would think the worse of him for it. If our shame-worthiness lies in the space between who we are and how we present ourselves to the world, Max was narrowing that gap to nothing. Whereas Jonah's gap was as wide as the Grand Canyon.

And Max had an ace up his sleeve. The *News of the World* had made a fatal mistake. The orgy was definitely German-tinged. But it was not Nazi-themed.

And so Max sued.

JAMES PRICE QC [Max Mosley's barrister]: I'm going to ask you to go through [the photographs] quite carefully with me, if you would. On page 291, nothing Nazi there?

COLIN MYLER [*News of the World* editor]: No.

PRICE: Page 292, that's Mr. Mosley having a cup of tea, nothing Nazi there?

MYLER: Correct.

PRICE: That is the SS style inspection sheet?

MYLER: Yes.

PRICE: You can quite clearly see from the photograph that it is a plastic spiral-bound notebook. I suggest to you that it is inconceivable that anybody could possibly honestly describe that as a SS style inspection sheet.

MYLER: I disagree.

PRICE: What do you know about medical examinations by the SS?

MYLER: I'm not a historian of them.

PRICE: Would it be fair to say you know nothing about SS medical inspections?

MYLER: Not in great detail, no.

PRICE: Anything at all?

MYLER: Not in great detail, no.

When Colin Myler and the paper's investigative journalist, Neville Thurlbeck, were asked in court to specify exactly where Max was mocking Jewish concentration-camp victims, they pointed to the photographs of the women guards shaving a naked Max and pointed out that Jews were shaved at concentration camps. But, as James Price QC indicated, they were shaving Max's bottom. That wasn't resonant of concentration camps at all. Furthermore, as Max explained during his evidence, if they'd wanted to look like Nazis, "it would have been easy to obtain Nazi uniforms online or from a costumier." Yes, there were uniforms, but they were generically German military.

The *News of the World*'s case crumbled further when an e-mail exchange between two of the women guards was read out in court.

Hi ladies. Just to confirm the scenario on Friday at
Chelsea starting at 3. If you're around before then, I'm
doing a judicial on him at noon so if you'd like to witness
that, be here for 11am but don't stress if you can't
make that.

Can't wait it'll be great . . . My bottom is so clear for a
change. Lots of love.

A "judicial"? A Nazi scenario might have been called a
"*Volksgerichtshof* trial" or maybe a *Gerichtsverfahren*. But a
judicial? James Price asked the *News of the World* to explain
why, if the orgy was so Nazi, one of the guards was constantly
referred to on the tape as "Officer Smith." They had no answer. Max won the case.

He won big: costs plus £60,000 in damages, the highest in
recent British legal history for a privacy case. And now, as
Max told me, people regard him "primarily as someone who
has been wronged and who has pushed rather successfully for
certain things. I'm a lot better off than I would have been if
I'd gone off to hide."

Within three years, the *News of the World* was no more. In
July 2011, *The Guardian* revealed that a private investigator
working for the paper had hacked into the voice mail of a
murdered teenager, Milly Dowler. In an attempt to control
the scandal, Rupert Murdoch shut the paper down. Later,
Neville Thurlbeck pled guilty to phone hacking and was imprisoned for six months. Colin Myler wasn't implicated and
is currently the president and editor in chief of the New York
Daily News.

Max felt like he'd been fighting not only for himself but

also for the dead who preceded him. He meant people like
Ben Stronge. "He was an English chef living in northern
France, divorced, and he was a swinger. A man and a woman
from the *News of the World* swung by his place. He gave them
dinner, disappeared upstairs, and apparently came back
down wearing nothing but a pouch." Max paused. Then he
said, softly, "Pathos."

That was June 1992. When Ben Stronge discovered that
the people looking at him weren't swingers but *News of the
World* journalists, he started crying. He telephoned the
paper's editor, Patsy Chapman. According to Max, "He said,
'Please don't publish, because if you do, I'll never see my children again.' Well, they published anyway. They didn't give a
damn. So he killed himself."

Then there was Arnold Lewis. In the spring of 1978 the
News of the World decided to infiltrate sex parties in cara-
vans in the forests of Wales. The journalist Tina Dalgleish
and her photographer, Ian Cutler, answered a small ad in a
swingers' magazine. It had been placed by a lay preacher and
teacher, Arnold Lewis. They met in the local pub.

The turnout was small. Five people showed up, three of
whom were Tina Dalgleish, Ian Cutler, and Arnold Lewis.
Arnold left a coded note for potential latecomers with an
arrow pointing in the direction of the caravan and the exact
walking distance: "3.8 miles."

At the caravan they drank sherry and ate biscuits, and an
orgy occurred (which Ian Cutler and Tina Dalgleish witnessed but didn't participate in), and then a few days later
Tina Dalgleish telephoned Arnold to reveal her identity.

Later, after I left Max, I managed to get Tina Dalgleish's

photographer on the phone. Ian Cutler was recovering from a major stroke, but he wanted to talk. He'd never stopped thinking about Arnold Lewis, he said. For thirty-five years it had plagued him.

"Arnold told Tina that if she published the story he would kill himself," Ian said. "He was a preacher. Fucking hell. He was a preacher in a small Welsh village."

The *News of the World* published and Arnold Lewis killed himself. He inhaled exhaust fumes. His body was found in his car the morning the story appeared. The headline read "If You Go Down to the Woods Today You're Sure of a Big Surprise."

• • •

Max and I spent the afternoon trying to work it out. There was something about his behavior in the aftermath of the *News of the World* story that made the public totally uninterested in annihilating him. He just naturally seemed to get the formula right. People melted. But what was it?

At one point he raised with me the possibility that he might be a sociopath. Maybe he'd survived it all by drawing on special sociopathic powers. Maybe his instantaneous "whoosh" of resilient fury at the newsstand was a sociopathic whoosh. Maybe that was what we liked about him—that resilient fury. He told me that in 1991, two years before getting the job as president of motor racing's governing body, they "commissioned a psychiatrist to analyze me, and the man concluded I was a sociopath." As he said this, he gave me an anxious glance.

I sighed.

"Do you feel empathy?" I asked him.

"*Yes!*" he said. "The motive of most of the main things I've done in my life is feeling sorry for people. And the psychiatrist never met me. He just did it from the outside."

"Well, I don't think you're a sociopath," I said.

"Phew!" said Max.

"Anyway," I said, "a psychologist once told me that if you're worried you may be a sociopath that means you aren't one."

"Thanks, Ron, another phew," Max replied. He paused. "Jon," he said, "I meant Jon."

"More proof you're not a sociopath, because sociopaths wouldn't care about calling me Ron," I said.

"Another phew!" said Max.

*   *   *

I t was getting dark by the time I left Max's house. We both felt we hadn't quite managed to solve the mystery, so we agreed to keep thinking about it.

"Oh, by the way," I said, on my way out. "Have you heard of an S&M place in America called Kink? I think I've got an invitation to visit them."

"Kink?" said Max. His eyes widened. "That is *the* place! I've only seen it on the Internet. They've got machines. They've got electrics. They've got water. You name it, they've got it. I'm quite envious!"

"Exciting!" I said.

My invitation to Kink.com had come about after I'd mentioned on Twitter that I was writing a book on public shaming. One of my followers—his name is Conner Habib—asked me if I was going to meet people who derive sexual pleasure from being publicly shamed.

"No!" I replied. "That hadn't crossed my mind at all."

He said that as it happened he was a gay porn star and if I wanted to know more about his work I should google him. I did and immediately saw many close-ups of his anus. I e-mailed him to ask how he managed to do that kind of work without feeling embarrassed.

"I do think there's lots to learn from porn stars about how not to be embarrassed or feel vulnerable," he e-mailed back. He added that a lot of sex industry people go on to become hospice workers: "They're not freaked out by the body, so they can help people transition through illness and death. I'm not sure what would humiliate me at this point. If you want to talk at length about this, I'm open to it. Just don't make me seem any goofier than I already am. Maybe that's what could humiliate a porn star—a Jon Ronson essay?"

I frowned.

Conner's e-mails got me interested in journeying into the porn world. Was it really populated by people who had learned how to be immune to shame? It suddenly seemed like a good talent to have.

He put me in touch with a famous porn impresario—

Princess Donna Dolore of Kink.com studios. We swapped e-mails. "Growing up I was ashamed of everything," she wrote, "and at a certain point I realized that if I was open with the world about the things that embarrassed me they no longer held any weight! I felt set free!" She added that she always derives her porn scenarios from this formula. She imagines circumstances that would mortify her, "like being bound naked on a street with everybody looking at you," and enacts them with like-minded porn actors, robbing them of their horror.

Donna and I arranged to have dinner in Los Angeles. That morning I e-mailed her: "See you tonight at 7 p.m.!"

At 5:40 p.m. I e-mailed her again, "Don't forget we're supposed to be meeting in an hour and twenty minutes!"

"Sure!" she replied.

I arrived at the restaurant at 6:50 p.m. Two hours and ten minutes later, still sitting there, I checked her Twitter feed. Her last message, written four hours earlier, read: "Somebody please tell me what the fuck I am supposed to do at 7 p.m.! Why the fuck don't I write this shit down?!?"

I trudged miserably back to my hotel. *If keeping people waiting in restaurants for hours is what it's like to live in a post-shame world,* I thought, *give me a bit of shame.*

At midnight Donna e-mailed me: "FUCK! I'm SO sorry."

"That's FINE!" I e-mailed back.

"There's a public disgrace tomorrow if you want to come," she e-mailed.

• • •

I t was midnight outside a sports bar in the San Fernando Valley. From the front, the place looked dark and empty—all shuttered up. But Donna had told me to go around the back to the fire door behind the bins. When Max had told me how impressive Kink.com was, he didn't mean the sports bar. Kink.com headquarters is a giant, ornate 1914 armory in San Francisco, equipped with all sorts of dungeon and torture equipment. I knocked on the fire door. A security guard ticked me off a list.

I scanned the barroom. There were twenty people in there—middle-aged men sitting alone, some young couples. Everyone looked nervous. A man walked over to me.

"I'm Shylar," he said. "Shylar Cobi."

"Are you a porn person?" I asked him.

"Twenty-three years," he said. "It's all I know."

He had a sweet, melancholy face. He reminded me of Droopy.

I asked him a bit about his life. He said he didn't just work with Donna. He was a producer for hire, averaging fifty porn shoots a year. Which meant he had a thousand credits in all, including—I later discovered on IMDb—*Orgy University*, *Wet Sweaty Boobs*, and *My Slutty Friends*.

"So what's the plan for tonight?" I asked him.

Shylar shrugged. "Same as always. They fuck, he finishes, we clean up, everyone goes home."

He gently squeezed my arm to make sure I was okay. He wasn't the only one. Various members of the production crew kept doing it to me all night—rubbing my back, squeezing my arm. I suppose, being tweedy and owl-like, I just don't look like the sort of person who normally hangs around extreme porn shoots, and I think everyone wanted to ensure that I was not feeling intimidated or about to faint. It was sweet. Porn professionals were being so nice and considerate toward me that it was almost as if *I* were the person about to have his genitals electrocuted. But it wasn't to be my genitals. It was to be the genitals of the porn actor Jodi Taylor, who was sitting in the corner of the bar discussing logistics with Princess Donna, who now stood up, hushed everyone, and made a speech about what was expected of us.

"So," she began. "The name of the site is Public Disgrace. It's a site about public humiliation. You guys are all just people drinking and having a good time, and you have no idea that we're going to be turning up at this bar. When we come in, you're all invited to participate to a certain extent. You can grope the model, assuming you have clean hands and short-filed fingernails. We have nail clippers and nail files if anyone thinks they're going to need them. You can smack her ass, but this is not about you showing us how hard you can smack someone. I don't want to see anyone take full swings. Sometimes people try and show off with their spanking. I'm sure you guys can all spank very, very hard, but I don't want to see it. Other things you can do. You can spit on her body. You can pour your drinks on her. You can pull her hair. You can gently smack her in the face. But try not to be too obnoxious. You are totally welcome to shout things out and verbally degrade her. That is encouraged. But just don't be *that guy*." She summarized: "So. Don't get shitfaced, don't fist her ass, enjoy."

Donna and Jodi Taylor disappeared to a corridor outside, where Donna attached a ball and chain to Jodi. Donna gave a signal to the cameraman. He pressed record. And it began.

The drinkers feigned surprise at the sight of Donna pulling a shrieking Jodi Taylor into the bar. "What *IS* going on?" said a man in a beanie hat. He slammed down his drink in "outrage."

Donna ripped off Jodi Taylor's clothes and attached electrodes to her genitals.

"What are you DOING?" said the man. He seemed to be the only crowd member daring enough to improvise dialogue or simulate emotions of any sort.

"It's electricity," Donna said. "Do you want to shock her?"

"Do I want to SHOCK her?" he said. "I just came in to get a drink. Oh. Okay."

Donna handed him the remote control. He pressed the button. Nothing happened.

"Turn it off and turn it on again," said Donna. He did. Then he pressed the button. Jodi Taylor screamed.

(Later, during a break from filming, a few crowd members expressed doubt that there really was electricity coursing through the pads into Jodi Taylor's genitals, so one of them placed the pad against her hand and pressed the button and shrieked. Later still, I got an e-mail from Jodi Taylor: "Obviously if something like public disgrace happened to me in real life, it'd be extremely intense, horrifying and awful. But that's the beauty of porn. You can actually do these crazy things without actually doing them. It's all make-believe. It's pure fantasy and a fantasy is never humiliating or scary. It's awesome. Princess Donna is all about making the PORN GIRL'S fantasy come alive far more than the fantasy of the people viewing it. Only with her can you have a fantasy as taboo as gangbang or public disgrace and actually get to live it out while being completely safe and comfortable.")

Shylar Cobi had told me that the crowd was composed of friends and friends of friends, with one exception. A hired porn actor was mingling among us. And now he emerged and started having sex with Jodi Taylor. At this, everyone became a bit bolder, if still slightly stilted. "Put ice on her tooth," a man shouted. Someone poured beer over Jodi Taylor's head. I tried to maintain a respectful distance, but from time to time, when needing to ensure that I was accurately chronicling the minutiae of it, I think I drifted into shot. And so, if you are a Public Disgrace viewer and the erotic ambience was ruined for you by the sudden emergence of a bespectacled man peering in close and writing things in a notepad, I'm sorry.

Then they finished and cleaned up, and everyone went home. Later I spent a little time with Donna. I told her I thought she'd definitely created a more mindful working environment than most regular offices. There were no bullying bosses stalking around shaming the employees. "Are other corners of the porn industry more frightening and exploitative?" I asked her. "And that's why everyone here was making a special effort?"

Donna nodded but said she didn't want to talk about other parts of the porn industry. She wanted to talk about what she was trying to achieve with Public Disgrace. "America is a very puritanical place," she said. "If I can help one person feel less freakish and alone because of what they like, then I'll be a success. But I know I've already reached more people than that."

. . .

A few weeks passed. And then I received an interesting e-mail from Max Mosley. Like me, he'd been thinking a lot about what it was about him that had helped him to stave off even the most modest public shaming. And now, he wrote, he thought he had the answer. It was simply that he had refused to feel ashamed.

"As soon as the victim steps out of the pact by refusing to feel ashamed," he said, "the whole thing crumbles."

I reread Max's e-mail. Could that be it? Does a shaming only work if the shamee plays his or her part in it by feeling ashamed? There was no doubt that Jonah, and Justine too, had been having intense conversations with their shame. Whereas Max was just refusing to engage with his at all. I wondered: Was unashamedness something that some people just had? Or was it something that could be taught?

And that was how I discovered a man teaching a course in how to refuse to feel ashamed.

Eight

The Shame-Eradication Workshop

Twelve Americans—strangers to one another—sat in a circle in a room in the JW Marriott hotel in Chicago. There were buttoned-down, preppy-looking businessmen and businesswomen, a young Burning Man–type drifter couple, a man with a Willie Nelson ponytail and deep lines in his face. In the middle sat Brad Blanton. He was a large man. His shirt, open to his chest, was yellow-white, like his hair. With his sunburned face, he looked like a red ball abandoned in dirty snow.

Now he stirred. "To begin," he said, "I want you to tell us something that you don't want us to know."

. . .

Alot of people move around in life chronically ashamed of how they look, or how they feel, or what they said, or what they did. It's like a permanent adolescent concern. Adolescence is when you're permanently concerned about what other people think of you."

It was a few months earlier, and Brad Blanton and I were talking on Skype. He was telling me about how, as a psychotherapist, he had come to understand how so many of us "live our lives constantly in fear of being exposed or being judged as immoral or not good enough."

But Brad had invented a way for us to eradicate those feelings, he told me. His method was called "Radical Honesty."

[Brad Blanton] says we should toss out the filters between our brains and our mouths. If you think it, say it. Confess to your boss your secret plans to start your own company. If you're having fantasies about your wife's sister, Blanton says to tell your wife and tell her sister. It's the only path to authentic relationships. It's the only way to smash through modernity's soul-deadening alienation.

—A. J. JACOBS, "I THINK YOU'RE FAT,"
Esquire, JULY 24, 2007

Brad's thinking was that shame grows when we internalize shame. Just look at the frantically evasive Jonah. Whereas look at Max Mosley. Brad's favorite animal was a dog. A dog doesn't lie. A dog doesn't feel shame. A dog lives in the moment. Max Mosley was like a dog. We should be like dogs. And our first step toward being like dogs was to reveal to the group something about ourselves that we really didn't want people to know.

By coincidence, a friend of mine, the writer and broadcaster Starlee Kine, took Brad's course a few years ago for a book she was writing. I met Starlee before I flew to Chicago. I told her not to tell me what to expect—I wanted to be surprised—but she did tell me the first part. She said it always begins with the participants' being asked to reveal a secret.

"With my group," Starlee told me, "the first man said that his secret was that he hadn't paid taxes in ten years. Everyone nodded and looked disappointed that his secret wasn't so sensational. Then the next man said that his secret was that he had once murdered a man. He was in a truck with a man, and he punched him in his head and threw him out, and the guy was dead, and another car ran him over. And he didn't go to jail and he never told anyone."

"What did Brad Blanton say?" I asked her.

"He said, 'Next. Great.' So then it got to the next woman. She said, 'Oh! My secrets are so boring! I suppose I can talk about how I have sex with my cat.' Then the murderer raised his hand and said, 'Excuse me. I'd like to add something to my secret. I'd like to add that I also have sex with my cat.'"

Starlee had found Brad's course crazy. I probably would have too had I not been seasoned in the destruction of Jonah and Justine and the salvation of Max.

"Well," began a woman called Melissa, sitting opposite me in the circle. Melissa was a successful lawyer. But her passion was sadomasochistic sex. "Humiliation is my biggest turn-on," she said. She has even built herself her own private dungeon. But Melissa's sex dungeon wasn't her secret. Her secret is that she earned more than $550,000 last year and felt ashamed to have earned so much.

Later, when I recounted this to Starlee, she explained to me that Melissa is actually a regular at Brad's workshops. She's Brad's protégée.

"Melissa tells everyone about her dungeon," Starlee said. "How you respond to it is her way of judging how enlightened you are."

Vincent sat next to Melissa. His secret was that he was beginning to regret signing up for Brad's course. "It was a snap decision and $500 is lot of money for me," he said. "I was going to spend it on visiting my girlfriend in Thailand."

"Has he paid in full?" Brad asked Melissa.

"Only the $150 deposit," Melissa replied.

"Get his money," Brad said to Melissa.

Brad was making the radically honest statement that he was more concerned about getting the $350 Vincent owed him than assuring Vincent that he'd made a good decision signing up for the course.

"Can I pay you what I owe you in the break?" Vincent asked.

Brad shot Vincent a suspicious glance.

Emily spoke next. Her secret was that she sells marijuana for a living.

"Like by the ounce?" someone asked her.

"By the pound," she replied. "I charge about $3,400 a pound."

"Are you worried about being caught?" I asked her.

"No," she said.

"We're very discreet," Emily's boyfriend, Mario, told the room.

Mario's secret was that he sometimes tells Emily he thinks she's fat.

"You're not fat," I said to Emily.

Mario's other secret is "I use my lucid dreams as opportunities to rape women. I find the first girl that's around and I do whatever I want. I have my way with her."

"Can I be the star of your next dream?" said Melissa.

I had a headache. "Does anyone have any headache tablets?" I asked the room. Melissa reached into her pocket and pulled out a little baggie filled with loose pills of different shapes and colors. She picked out two and handed them to me. I swallowed them.

"Thank you," I said. "I have no idea what kind of pills you just gave me. It actually crossed my mind that you might have just given me a date rape drug."

Wow, what a good feeling! I thought. *I thought it so I said it, with no possibility of negative consequences!*

Melissa glanced inscrutably at me.

Jim was an engineer for an oil company.

"I don't want you guys to know . . ." Jim's voice cracked. ". . . that I am a drug addict."

He made this declaration with such quiet power that it took the room aback.

"They don't drug-test you at your oil company?" someone asked Jim.

"Yes, they do," Jim replied.

"You don't flunk it?" asked Brad.

"No," said Jim. "I haven't flunked it yet."

"How do you get around it?" asked Brad's friend Thelma, whose secret was that she watches gay male porn.

"I . . . don't know," Jim said.

"What drugs are you addicted to?" Brad asked Jim.

"I like . . . marijuana," Jim said.

There was a short silence. "How much do you smoke?" I asked him.

"In three weeks I'll smoke an ounce of marijuana," said Jim.

"Is that *it*?" screeched Emily.

"I was once very attracted to a man I thought was a woman and ended up spending time with him and paying for that time," Jim said.

Everyone looked a little less underwhelmed at Jim's new secret.

Mary's secret was how badly she was taking being rejected by her partner, Amanda. "I'm fifty and I'm alone," Mary said. She looked at the floor. "I've lost myself."

Mary wasn't just sitting around moping at home. It was worse than that. She was repeatedly telephoning Amanda. There was a time when Amanda would say to Mary, "One day I'll marry you." Now all Amanda was telling her was, "Stop calling me."

Brad told Mary to take the Hot Seat. He pointed to an empty chair.

"What would you say to Amanda if she was sitting opposite you right now?" Brad asked her.

"I'd tell her that I resent her for saying don't contact me."

"Say it to her," said Brad.

"I resent you for saying, 'Don't call me,'" Mary said quietly into space.

"See what it feels like to use an angry voice," Brad said.

"FUCK YOU," Mary yelled at the empty chair. "I resent you for saying, 'One day I'm going to marry you,' and then you didn't. So FUCK YOU. I resent you because you're such a fucking bitch sometimes. I resent you for treating me like . . . I resent you for saying all those beautiful things and you took them all back . . ." Mary was sobbing.

"Good," Brad said. "When are you going to say this to her face?"

Mary swallowed. "I'm wondering at what location . . ."

"Call her up," Brad told her. "Say, 'It's not a request. We're either going to do this alone or in front of your whole goddamned office and you've got one day to make up your fucking mind.'"

"Okay," said Mary, quietly.

"So, when?" Brad said.

"By next weekend?" Mary said.

"Good," Brad said.

Jack, a veterinarian sex addict, looked uneasy. "How do you put this approach in the context of people not calling the police?" he asked Brad.

"You're asking people to leave this session," I agreed, "and do something to people who aren't part of this. People must get hurt. The police must get called sometimes."

"People call the police sometimes." Brad shrugged. "It takes twenty minutes for the police to get there. So you've got twenty minutes to complete all your anger."

"I can't imagine this always works out well," I said.

"That's because you've been brainwashed your entire life about all the terrible things that are going to happen," Brad said. "Yeah, people get mad. People get upset. But people get over stuff. People worry about what happens in the first five seconds. But I'm concerned about the next five minutes. I'm committed to people staying with each other until they get over this."

This last part, Brad said, was critical. You remain with the person you've just been yelling at until the resentments fizzle. That's how wounds heal.

Vincent—the man who was regretting signing up for the course—suddenly announced, "I'm sorry. I'm leaving. This isn't for me. I'm sorry."

"I resent you for saying you're leaving," said Melissa.

"Okay," said Vincent.

"I don't think I'll ever get over this resentment," said Melissa.

Wow, I thought. Give the man a break. She's only just met him. "I resent you telling him that you'll never get over the resentment of him leaving," I told Melissa.

"I appreciate you for sitting there listening to me," Melissa said to Vincent.

"Thank you," Vincent said.

"Shit or get off the pot, man," said Jack the veterinarian sex addict. "I resent you for saying you're leaving and I resent that you're still here."

Vincent left.

The day's session ended. I said I hoped nobody minded but I was tired so I wasn't going to have dinner with the group. I was just going to watch TV and send some e-mails instead.

"I feel slighted," said Brad.

"Ach, no you don't," I said. Although I knew that he did.

• • •

There was a reason I needed to go to my room that I hadn't explained to anyone. I had a work crisis. A story I'd been working on had turned chaotic, and my editor and I were at loggerheads, sending each other tense e-mails.

It had sounded like an intriguing story at the beginning. There has been a tradition over the years of journalists wearing disguises to experience injustice firsthand. The pioneer was John Howard Griffin, who in 1959 stained his skin dark and spent six weeks hitchhiking as a black man through the segregated Deep South—a journey chronicled in his 1961 book *Black Like Me*. From time to time, editors have asked me to undertake similar journeys. After 9/11, a TV producer suggested I stain my own skin and move into a Muslim area of London. But it seemed to me like she basically wanted me to spy on Muslims, so I said no. This time, however, I'd been asked to disguise myself to experience a different injustice.

"We want you to be a woman," the editor had said. "We'll work with a prosthetics artist to make you unrecognizable. We'll get a movement coach to teach you how to walk like a woman."

"Women and men walk differently?" I asked.

"Yes," she said.

"I never knew that," I said. "This could be really interesting. As a man, I'm rarely stared at lasciviously. But as a woman, I might get stared at lasciviously a lot. How would that make me *feel*? And do women behave differently when there are no men around—like at women-only gyms and women-only saunas? I'm intrigued. I'll do it."

So I met with a prosthetics artist at a college in West London. She encased my face in alginate and took a cast. A prosthetic mask was made. She spent a couple of weeks manipulating it into womanly features. I slipped it over my face. I looked like a woman with a gigantic head. The editor called me in for a meeting.

"It's fine," she said. "Don't worry. We won't use the prosthetic head. We can still make you look exactly like a woman."

"Are you sure?" I said.

"You'll be amazed what a few hours with the movement coach will do," she said.

"You don't think we're in danger of relying too much on the movement coach?" I said. "It had been the prosthetics that had rather sold me on the idea."

"I promise you that we won't let you out of this building unless you absolutely pass as a woman," she said.

So, in an empty conference room in a quiet corner of the magazine's offices, I dressed as a woman. Makeup was applied. I put on a wig and a dress and a padded bra. I spent hours under the tutelage of the movement coach. Test photographs were taken. Finally, I left the conference room and walked toward the editor's desk in the manner that the movement coach had instructed.

She swallowed slightly when she saw me.

"They've done an incredible job," she said. She turned to the deputy editor. "Haven't they done an amazing job?"

The deputy editor swallowed slightly. "Yes," she said.

"You look exactly like a woman," said the editor. "Now go outside and experience life as a woman."

"I don't think I look like a woman," I said.

"What are you talking about?" said the editor. "You look *exactly* like a woman."

"I don't think I look anything like a woman," I said.

She peered at my tormented facial expression.

I hesitated for a moment. Then I walked toward the exit. Sweat smudged my foundation. I glanced back over my shoulder at the editors. They were giving me encouraging looks and indicating the door. I felt sick, short of breath. My stomach muscles clenched.

And then I stopped. I couldn't do it. I turned, went back downstairs, and I put on my male clothes.

A week had passed and our relationship remained frosty. She felt I had prevaricated unprofessionally and was acting too sensitive. "Don't over-think it, Jon," she'd e-mailed me. "It's just a fun feature. Shouldn't be the cause of some sort of a midlife crisis." I felt that the story's original premise had fallen to pieces and the reason they were happy to send me out into the world looking nothing like a woman was that in our line of work the more humiliated a person is, the more viral the story tends to go. Shame can factor large in the life of a journalist—the personal avoidance of it and the professional bestowing of it onto others.

Nobody must ever see those test pictures, I'd been thinking all week. *Never.*

Now, as I lay in my hotel room, I understood the truth of it. My terror of humiliation had closed a door. Great adventures that might have unfolded involving me dressed as a woman would never now unfold. I'd been constrained by the terror. It had blown me off course. Which, actually, meant that I was

just like the vast majority of people. I knew this from studying the work of David Buss, a professor of evolutionary psychology at the University of Texas at Austin.

One day in the early 2000s Buss was at a cocktail party
when the wife of a friend began flirting with another man in
front of everyone: "She was a striking woman," Buss later
wrote. "She looked at her husband derisively and made a
derogatory remark about the way he looked, then turned
right back to her flirtatious conversation."

Buss's friend stomped outside, where Buss found him
fuming, saying he felt humiliated and wanted to kill his wife:
"I had no doubt that he would do it. In fact, he was so wild
with rage, such a transformed man, he seemed capable of
killing any living thing within an arm's reach. I became
frightened for my own life."

Buss's friend didn't kill his wife. He calmed down. But the
incident shook Buss up. Which was why he decided to carry
out an experiment. He asked five thousand people a question:
Had they ever fantasized about killing someone?

"Nothing," as Buss later wrote in his book *The Murderer
Next Door*, "prepared me for the outpouring of murderous
thoughts."

It turned out from his survey that 91 percent of men and
84 percent of women had experienced "at least one vivid fantasy of killing someone." There was the man who imagined
"hiring an explosives specialist" to blow his boss up in his
car, the woman who wanted to "break every bone" in her
partner's body, "starting with his fingers and toes, then slowly
making my way to larger ones." There was a bludgeoning

with a baseball bat, a strangling followed by a beheading, a stabbing during sex. Some people were set on fire. One man was exposed to killer bees.

"Murderers are waiting," Buss's book bleakly concludes. "They are watching. They are all around us."

Buss's findings deeply distressed him. But I saw them as good news. Surely fantasizing about killing someone and then not doing it is a way we teach ourselves to be moral. So Buss's conclusions seemed silly to me. But there was something different about his study that I found extraordinary. It was something that—as Buss's research assistant Joshua Duntley e-mailed me—"we did not code for specifically." It was the part where Buss asked them what had stimulated their murderous thoughts.

There was the boy who daydreamed about kidnapping his schoolmate, "breaking both his legs so he couldn't run, beating him until his insides were a bloody pulp, then I'd tie him to a table and drip acid onto his forehead." What had the schoolmate done to him? "He 'accidentally' dropped his books on my head and all his friends had a good laugh." There was the office worker who imagined "tampering with my boss's car brakes so he'd have a braking failure on the motorway." Why? "He had given me the impression that I was a real loser. He would mock me in front of other people. I felt humiliated."

And on it went. Almost none of the murderous fantasies were dreamed up in response to actual danger—stalker ex-boyfriends, etc. They were all about the horror of humiliation. Brad Blanton was right. Shame internalized can lead to agony. It can lead to Jonah Lehrer. Whereas shame let out can lead to freedom, or at least to a funny story, which is a sort of freedom too.

And so there in my room I decided that on day two of Brad's course I would go for it. I would let the shame out. I would be Max Mosley. I would be radically honest.

· · ·

On day two of Brad's course, Brad asked me in front of the group if I'd like to take the Hot Seat, given that I'd been so quiet on day one.

I cleared my throat. Everyone was smiling expectantly at me as if I were the start of a good television program.

I hesitated.

"Actually, I won't," I said.

The expectant smiles turned quizzical.

"The truth is," I explained, "I don't think my problems are as bad as everyone else's problems in the room. Plus, I don't like conflict."

I clarified that I wasn't against conflict in a *weird* way: I quite enjoy watching other people being in conflict. If I notice two people yelling at each other on the street, I would often stop at a distance and have a look. But it just wasn't my thing to *participate* in conflict.

"So I don't want people to think I'm anti–Hot Seat," I concluded. "They've been my favorite parts of the course so far. I find the lectures in between them quite boring but the Hot Seats are great."

"So you want there to be a Hot Seat but you don't want to be the one to get in it?" said Brad's friend Thelma.

"Yes," I said.

"I say do a Hot Seat right now, go ahead and get in it," Thelma said.

"No, no," I said again. "I'm honestly more comfortable watching other people do it."

"CHICKEN SHIT!" Thelma yelled. "I call CHICKEN SHIT! If you get a chance to jump on Jon, do."

"Ha-ha," I said. "But seriously, I've got nothing that's so pressing for me to be in the Hot Seat. I don't want an awkward silence and I don't want to dredge something up. I'd be faking it. I just think other people here have got more issues than I do."

"BULLSHIT!" yelled Thelma.

"YOU'RE AN ARROGANT CONDESCENDING BASTARD!" said Brad.

"I don't think I said anything condescending," I said, surprised.

"'You people need it and I don't,'" said Brad, impersonating me.

"I actually really resent you for saying that," said Jack, the veterinarian with the sex addiction. "It was FUCKING condescending. I also resent that you're sitting there fiddling with that fucking phone constantly, which I find extremely distracting. I RESENT YOU FOR HOLDING THE PHONE!"

"Can I say something about the phone . . . ?" I said.

"We don't give a fuck what your reason is," said Brad. "We're going to resent you whether you explain it or not."

"That's not how conversations work," I said.

"Jon, do you have a resentment you want to share about anyone in this room?" said Melissa, hopefully.

I paused. "No," I said.

"I JUST WANT YOU TO KNOW THAT YOU'RE A BULLSHIT ARTIST AND EVERYTHING YOU'RE SAYING IS BULLSHIT," yelled Brad.

"RIGHT," I screeched. "I resent YOU"—I glared at Jack— "for saying I'm condescending. I'm NOT condescending. I was basing my opinion that your problems are worse than mine ENTIRELY on the things you've all SAID IN THIS ROOM. And I resent YOU"—I looked at Thelma—"for acting like Brad's stooge, like his gang member. There is nothing I dislike more in the world than people who care more about ideology than they do about people. You swamped me with a tidal wave of Brad's ideology."

"THAT'S A STORY YOU'VE MADE UP ABOUT ME!" shouted Thelma. "Yeah? He wants to tell me, 'FUCKING BACK OFF,' but he's afraid of the conflict! So his mind kicks in!"

"I resent you for repeatedly yelling 'Chicken shit' and 'Bullshit' at me because . . ." I said.

"Not 'because,'" said Thelma. "That's interpretive."

I stared openmouthed at Thelma. She was COACHING me? In fact—it dawned on me—none of the yelling was a break from their therapeutic milieu. It was Radical Honesty. It works wonders for some of Brad's clients. But it wasn't working wonders for me. I was beginning to feel intensely rageful.

"Do you resent me for telling you what to say?" said Thelma.

"Yes, I fucking do," I yelled. "I massively fucking resent you for telling me what to say."

"Poor little thing," said Brad. "We're so sorry we hurt your tender little feelings. Okay!" Brad clapped his hands together. "Lunch! I hate to abandon you, Jon, but I'm going to leave you cooking."

The group stood up and began drifting away.

They were breaking for lunch?

"But I'm still very resentful," I said.

"Good!" said Brad. "I hope you remain incomplete all lunch."

"I don't see any value in that at all," I muttered, as I put on my jacket.

Out in the hotel corridor Mario the marijuana dealer smiled and told me, "I don't think Brad's finished with you yet!" I understood why Mario said that. Brad seemed to have just broken his own golden rule. He hadn't ensured that everyone stayed together while my anger played itself out. No love had been given the chance to grow. I had been cast out into Chicago at an apex of resentfulness.

I spent the lunch hour stomping around the streets. After lunch, I had only a few hours before I needed to catch my plane back to New York, so I laid out for Brad my complaint.

"You broke for lunch right in the middle of it," I said. "You left me seething."

Melissa leaned over and removed my baseball cap from my head. I flinched.

"I could have been suicidally unhappy about it," I said.

"We were running ten minutes late for lunch, so I made the decision to leave you cooking," Brad said.

After that, things moved on. Jack the veterinarian sex addict who hated my fiddling with my phone took the Hot Seat. He recounted a time his father physically attacked his mother in front of him. It was a heartbreaking story. He closed his eyes tightly as he told it, so I took the opportunity to quickly check Twitter. I hate not knowing what's happening on Twitter. Soon after that, I caught my plane home.

We all kept in touch for a while. Mary e-mailed me to let me know how things had gone with Amanda: "I tried the Rad. Hon. approach and she was super resistant and defensive and pretty much closed to what I wanted to express. I could feel the waves of anger coming off her while talking to her. Since then I have had to still see her at the gym and at times I've 'ignored' her. Other times we've had civil, pleasant chats (not that many)."

Another member of the group e-mailed us all to report that he attempted Radical Honesty on his wife, but she responded by trying to physically push him away so he told her that he would "'get the ax and defend myself by killing you.' Rightfully she was scared, as she knows that often I confuse truth with fantasy. We all do. So the police came by. I am under consideration for a job that involves a security clearance, so any ARREST will result in no offer there . . . I love you all, especially Thelma, who I find extremely attractive, and I want to have sex with her (you). Perhaps I could even treat her (you) as my wife."

Brad wrote back, copying everyone in: "What you say is

completely insane. Your best bet is to seek out a psychiatrist who can prescribe you a mild tranquilizer."

My Radical Honesty weekend had not been a success for me. But I continued to believe that Max Mosley's own version of it—*"as soon as the victim steps out of the pact by refusing to feel ashamed, the whole thing crumbles"*—had indeed been his magic formula, the reason why he'd soared above his shaming. And I continued to believe it right up until a new public shaming unfolded, this time up in Kennebunk, Maine, that forced me to rethink the whole thing. This new shaming made me realize that Max had survived his for a completely different reason—one I hadn't put my finger on.

Nine

A Town Abuzz over Prostitution and a Client List

KENNEBUNK, Me.—The summer people who clog the roads here are long gone and the leaves have turned crimson and orange, but the prevailing sentiment in this postcard-perfect coastal town these days is one of dread.

For more than a year, the police have been investigating reports that the local Zumba instructor [Alexis Wright] was using her exercise studio on a quaint downtown street for more than fitness training. In fact, the police say, she was running a one-woman brothel with up to 150 clients and secretly videotaping them as they

engaged in intimate acts . . . the list is rumored to be replete with the names of prominent people.

—KATHARINE Q. SEELYE, *The New York Times*,
OCTOBER 16, 2012

President George H. W. Bush has his seaside compound,
Walker's Point, four miles away from Kennebunk, up in
Kennebunkport. Sometimes blacked-out cars zoom through
town on their way up there, carrying Vladimir Putin or Bill
Clinton or Nicolas Sarkozy, but besides that, not much hap-
pens in Kennebunk. Or not much did.

Who might be on the list? A member of the Bush family?
Someone from the Secret Service? General Petraeus?

—BETHANY MCLEAN, "TOWN OF WHISPERS,"
Vanity Fair, FEBRUARY 1, 2013

A defense attorney, Stephen Schwartz, petitioned the
Maine Supreme Judicial Court to have the names on the list
remain secret (he was representing two of the unnamed
men). This was still Puritan country, he argued: "Once these
names are released, they're all going to have the mark of a
scarlet letter." But the judge ruled against him, and the *York
County Coast Star*, the Kennebunk paper, started publishing.
There were sixty-nine people on the list in all—sixty-eight
men and one woman. Sadly, no Bush was among them, not

even a member of the family's security detail. But there were Kennebunk society people—a pastor from the South Portland Church of the Nazarene, a lawyer, a high school hockey coach, a former town mayor, a retired schoolteacher and his wife.

This was a unique event in the public shaming world. Mass disgrace scenarios like this never happen. Given that my job had become to try matching personality nuances with public shaming survival levels, it was a dream come true for me. When do you get a sample size like that? Surely among the people on the list there'd be those so eager to please that they'd allow strangers' negative opinions of them to meld with their own, creating some corrosive amalgam. There'd be those so desperate not to lose their status that it would need to be pried from their clenched fingers. There'd be serious people like Jonah, hitherto smart-alecky people like Justine. And there'd be Max Mosleys. Kennebunk was like a well-stocked laboratory for me. Who would incur the crowd's wrath, who its mercy? Who'd be shattered? Who'd emerge unscathed? I drove up there.

Inside Court One of the Biddeford District Courthouse half a dozen of the men from the Zumba list sat on the benches, staring grimly ahead while news crews pointed their cameras at them. We in the press area were allowed to stare at them and they weren't able to look away. It reminded me of how Nathaniel Hawthorne had described the pillory in *The Scarlet Letter*: "[An] instrument of discipline, so fashioned as to confine the human head in its tight grasp, and thus hold it up to public gaze. The very ideal of ignominy was embodied and made manifest in this contrivance of wood and iron. There can be no outrage, methinks . . . more flagrant than to forbid the culprit to hide his face for shame."

Everyone was silent and a little awkward, like we were all standing around in some strange pre-consensus limbo. This story was new. There hadn't been time for Kennebunk society to start shunning the men. However brutal or subtle the shunning might manifest itself, nothing had happened yet. I was in on the ground floor.

The judge entered, and it began. The court proceedings were nothing much. The men were, in turn, told to stand up and plead guilty or not guilty. Each man pled guilty. Fines were imposed—$300 for each visit to Alexis Wright. The maximum fine today was $900. And then it was over. They were allowed to leave. And they did, hurriedly. I followed the last one out. All the others had vanished except for him. I introduced myself to him.

"You can interview me," he said. "But I want something in return."

"Okay?" I said.

"Money," he said. "I'm not talking about much. Just enough to buy my kid a present from Walmart. Just a voucher from Walmart. And then I'll tell you *all* the details. I'll tell you EVERYTHING. What me and Alexis got up to."

He was a heavy man. He gave me a look of desperate, sad, faux lasciviousness, like he was offering me the best erotic novel. "I'll tell you everything," he said.

I said I couldn't pay someone to talk about his or her crime, so he shrugged and walked away. I drove back to New

York and the next day I wrote to all sixty-eight men and one woman on the list, requesting interviews. Then I waited.

A few days later, an e-mail arrived.

Okay, we can talk. I am the former Church of the
Nazarene pastor that unfortunately became involved
in this whole mess.

Sincerely yours,
James (Andrew) Ferreira

. . .

Hello, Jon." Andrew Ferreira's voice was kind and tired and lost-sounding—a formerly chipper community leader trying to adapt to a world that might no longer have any interest in his leadership. This was the first time he'd agreed to talk to a journalist. He said the last few days had been hard. His wife had left him and he'd been fired from his job. All that had been inevitable, he said, but the rest was unknown. The extent to which the community would cast him out, and how he'd deal with it: unknown.

I asked him why he visited Alexis Wright.

"Maybe my marriage wasn't great," he replied. "It wasn't horrible. It was just sort of drifting. Cohabiting to a point. Anyway. I was reading a story in *The Boston Globe* on the Craigslist Killer. You remember that story? He murdered a twenty-something call girl. And *The Boston Globe* said that most of the ads for escorts have migrated away from Craigslist and onto Backpage.com. If someone wants an escort or a happy-ending massage or something—Backpage.com. And I just remembered it. I wish I hadn't. Unfortunately, some things just stick in your mind. I became tainted with the information."

Andrew visited Alexis three times, he said. On the last occasion "we shared a laugh. We both just belly laughed. That was outside of what I was there for. And she became human to me then. She was no longer an object. And that was the puncturing of the fantasy. It was anything I could do to get out of there. I'm not one to wear my emotions on my sleeve. But I bawled my eyes out in the car."

And that was his last visit to Alexis Wright.

"How have you been spending the past few days?" I asked him.

"I don't sit alone at home and isolate," he replied. "I've joined a meet-up group. It's just a bunch of people and I'm completely anonymized there. I show up and we play board games. Risk and Apples to Apples and Pandemic. Besides that, I've been journaling. What do I do with all this information? If I wait a little bit—six months, a year—and I try to send out a manuscript? Is that something that would be received?"

"Like a memoir?"

"Could I utilize that to springboard into a new ministry?" he said. "And what angle do I come at it at? I could go faith-based and warn men not to do it. Or I could take a completely different tack and, well, I don't want to become a champion for legalized prostitution. So I've really got to think about what this all means." He drifted off. "What do I do with this?" he said again. "I don't know yet. Unfortunately, I'm forty-nine years old and I've turned a great deal of my life into a cautionary tale . . ."

"Have you met any of the other men or the woman from the list?" I asked.

"No," he said. "We're all members of a club we didn't realize we were in. There's really no reason or opportunity for any contact or solidarity."

"So mainly you're just waiting for whatever happens next to happen," I said.

"Yeah," he said. "That's the worst. The expectation. It's horrible."

Andrew promised to let me know the moment his shaming began—online, in town, anywhere. At the first hint of it, he assured me, he'd call. We said our good-byes. And that was the last I heard from him for several months.

So I telephoned him again. He sounded happy to get my call.

"I never heard from you," I said. "What happened?"

"It went away," he said.

"There was no shaming at all?"

"None," he said. "My imagination had been far worse than what actually happened."

"Justine Sacco was annihilated," I said. "And Jonah Lehrer too, of course. But Justine Sacco! And she didn't do anything wrong! And you got *nothing*?"

"I don't have an answer for that," Andrew said. "I don't understand it. In fact, my relationship with my three daughters has never been stronger. My youngest one noted, 'It's like getting to know you all over again.'"

"Your transgression made them see you as human?" I said.

"Yeah," Andrew said.

"Huh," I said. "Justine's and Jonah's transgressions made people see them as the opposite of human."

His marriage was over, he added, as was his job as a pastor in the local Nazarene church. That wasn't coming back. But otherwise he had experienced only kindness and forgiveness. Actually, it wasn't kindness and forgiveness. It was something much better than that. It was *nothing*. He experienced *nothing*.

Andrew told me a story. When Alexis Wright's business partner, Mark Strong, was on trial for bankrolling the brothel, Andrew was ordered into court. There was a chance he'd be called as a witness, so he was sequestered in a private room at the back. After a while, six other men drifted into the room. They all nodded at each other but sat in silence. Then some tentative conversations ensued and they realized what they'd suspected: They were Alexis Wright's clients. They were all men from the list. This was the first time they'd met, so they hurriedly, quite eagerly, swapped notes. Not about their visits to Alexis—everyone tiptoed awkwardly around *that*—but about what had happened next, once they were outed.

"One man was saying, 'It cost me a new SUV for my wife,'" Andrew said. "Another said, 'It cost me a cruise to the Bahamas and a new kitchen.' Everyone was laughing."

"None of them had fallen victim to any kind of shaming?" I asked.

"No," said Andrew. "It went away for them too."

But there was one exception, Andrew said. The conversation between them turned to the one woman who had visited Alexis.

"Everyone was laughing about her," Andrew said. "Then, suddenly, this one older gentleman, who had been much quieter than the others, said, 'That was my wife.' Oh, Jon, you could feel the energy shift. Everything changed immediately."

"What kind of jokes had you all been making about the wife?" I asked.

"I don't remember exactly," Andrew said, "but they had been more mocking. She was looked at differently by the men and, yes, with her it was considered more shameful."

As it happens, Max's and Andrew's sins would in Puritan times have been judged graver than Jonah's. Jonah, "guilty of lying or publishing false news," would have been "fined, placed in the stocks for a period not exceeding four hours, or publicly whipped with not more than forty stripes," according to Delaware law. Whereas Max and Andrew, having "defiled the marriage bed," would have been publicly whipped (no maximum number was specified), imprisoned with hard labor for at least a year, and on a second offense, imprisoned for life.

But the shifting sands of shameworthiness had shifted away from sex scandals—if you're a man—to work improprieties and perceived white privilege, and I suddenly understood the real reason why Max had survived his shaming. *Nobody cared.* Max survived his shaming because he was a man in a consensual sex shaming—which meant there had been no shaming.

I e-mailed Max to tell him. *"Nobody cared!"* I wrote. "Of all the public scandals, being a man in a consensual sex scandal is probably the one to hope for." Max was a target of no one—not liberals like me, not the online misogynists who tear apart women who step out of line. Max suffered nothing.

An hour passed. Then Max e-mailed back: "Hi Ron. I think you are spot on."

• • •

It wasn't that *nobody* cared. Max's wife cared. And someone else did: Paul Dacre, the editor of the *Daily Mail*. In a 2008 speech to the Society of Editors, Paul Dacre called Max's orgy "perverted, depraved, the very abrogation of civilized behavior." It was a rueful speech lamenting the death of shame. Dacre portrayed Justice David Eady—the judge who found in Max's favor in the privacy case against the *News of the World*—as its incarnation.

> The judge found for Max Mosley because he had not engaged in a "sick Nazi orgy" as the *News of the World* contested, though for the life of me that seems an almost surreally pedantic logic as some of the participants were dressed in military-style uniform. Mosley was issuing commands in German while one prostitute pretended to pick lice from his hair, a second fellated him and a third caned his backside until blood was drawn . . . [To Justice Eady] such behavior was merely "unconventional." . . .

But what is most worrying about Justice Eady's decisions is that he is ruling that—when it comes to morality— the law in Britain is now effectively neutral, which is why I accuse him, in his judgments, of being "amoral."

Ever since I started telling people I was writing a book about shame, lots of people from the Paul Dacre–type world— successful older men high up in British society—have congratulated me, presumptuously, for telling it how it is about how young people don't feel shame anymore. I met a famous architect at a party who said just that. And a religious broadcaster bemoaned to me how the loosening of religious morality has created a shameless society. I can understand why someone might believe that, given that we're living in an age where a Church of the Nazarene pastor can visit a prostitute and nobody cares. I think Andrew and Max have women like Princess Donna to thank for their non-disgrace. Donna has worked assiduously for years to demystify strange sex, which is why men like them are able to emerge from their scandals unscathed. But shame hasn't died. Shame has just moved elsewhere, gathering tremendous strength along the way.

The fact was, speeches like Paul Dacre's didn't matter anymore. The people who mattered didn't care what Dacre thought. The people who mattered were the people on Twitter. On Twitter we make our own decisions about who deserves obliteration. We form our own consensus, and we aren't being influenced by the criminal justice system or the media. This makes us formidable.

My journey to find a shame-free paradise—somewhere

we can be safe from the likes of us—had been a failure. Radical Honesty felt to me like people just yelling at each other. Neither Max nor Andrew had helpful secrets to impart about mustering the strength to survive the agony of a shaming. For them, there had been no shaming to survive. In fact, the only place on my journey where I'd witnessed any form of post-shame enlightenment was the Public Disgrace shoot at the sports bar in the San Fernando Valley. I looked back on the night with fondness. It was the only place I'd been to since I started writing this book that had felt *relaxing*.

Then I reread my transcript of a conversation I'd had with Donna that night and saw something I hadn't noticed before.

> DONNA: I was just coming home from Sacramento. I was at the airport. And I read something about myself on TMZ.

TMZ is a celebrity-gossip website. When Donna read their story, she told me, she suddenly saw how she looked to the outside world. It made her feel deeply humiliated and upset.

> DONNA: I'd been in this bubble in San Francisco, surrounded by other sex-positive people who are knowledgeable about sex work, about the sex industry, and so I never felt judged. But then all of a sudden I had these people looking at me from the outside and talking about me as if I was some idiotic pornographer. It was really hard. I was crying at the airport. I was crying on the plane ride.

Now I hunted down the TMZ article. What had been so crushing? How brutal had they been about Donna?

> James Franco is working on a top secret project with an up-and-coming female porn director, TMZ has learned . . . and it turns out she has quite the reputation for being handy with her fist. The woman in the photo is Princess Donna Dolore, who's featured in Franco's soon-to-be released film "Kink." Despite being in the film, Franco only met PDD for the first time in person last week . . . and sources tell us he has already locked her up to be a part of a future project he is working on. During the encounter, PDD gave Franco an official Princess Donna Dolore shirt, which includes her trademark fist on the back. James took it . . . the shirt, that is . . . and sported it proudly. We reached out to Franco for comment—but so far, no word back.
>
> —TMZ STAFF, DECEMBER 26, 2012

Years ago I might have thought it crazy that Donna had become so upset over such an innocuous article. But now I understood. I think we all care deeply about things that seem totally inconsequential to other people. We all carry around with us the flotsam and jetsam of perceived humiliations that actually mean nothing. We are a mass of vulnerabilities, and who knows what will trigger them? And so I sympathized with Donna. It seemed sad—given how Max and Andrew owed her so much—that as soon as she saw herself from the outside she felt ashamed, like the shame had snaked its way into her and there was no escaping.

I'm sure there are psychopaths out there—people neurologically incapable of feeling shame, as if they were shrouded in layers of cotton wool—but I hadn't met anybody like that on this journey. Ever since I began writing this book, though, one name kept coming up as someone who had survived a public shaming with such an apparent lack of effort that he made the entire concept of public shame seem like no big deal. And now after some reluctant e-mails—"I hope you'll understand, I'm wary"—he had agreed to meet me for lunch. His name was Mike Daisey.

Ten

The Near Drowning of Mike Daisey

I t feels like they want an apology, but it's a lie." Mike Daisey and I were sitting in a Brooklyn restaurant. He was a big man and he frequently dabbed the perspiration from his face with a handkerchief that was always within his reach. "It's a lie because they don't want an apology," he said. "An apology is supposed to be a communion—a coming together. For someone to make an apology, someone has to be listening. They listen and you speak and there's an exchange. That's why we have a thing about accepting apologies. There's a power exchange that happens. But they don't want an apology." He looked at me. "What they want is my destruction. What they want is for me to die. They will never say this because it's too histrionic. But they never want to hear from me again for the rest of my life, and while they're never hearing from me, they have the right to use me as a cultural reference point whenever it services *their* ends. That's how it would work out best for *them*. They would like me to never speak again." He paused. "I'd never had the opportunity to be the object of hate before. The hard part isn't the hate. It's the object."

Mike Daisey's transgression—which was remarkably similar to Jonah's—had been uncovered three months before Michael Moynihan lay on his sofa that July Fourth and wondered when Bob Dylan had ever called the creative process "just the sense that you got something to say." Like Jonah and Stephen Glass, Mike Daisey had been caught lying in a story. His was about a trip he had just taken to Shenzhen, China, during which he met factory workers who made Apple products. But some of the meetings had never happened. His shaming was maybe even more agonizing than Jonah's because every breath of it—every long, panicked silence—was captured on audio and broadcast on one of America's most popular radio shows, *This American Life*. Mike Daisey has always been a dandy. He was a big, loud, flamboyant character in New York's theater world. And for much of the broadcast, he sounded like he thought he could bluster his way through it. He had hope. He made justifications and nitpicked little points. But as the hour unfolded, it all crumbled, and by the end, when he finally said, "I'm sorry," he sounded finished— exhausted, empty. It was such an agonized "I'm sorry" that I thought there was a chance he would leave the radio studio, go home, and kill himself. But instead, within minutes, he published an apologetic statement on his website, and by the next day, he was back on Twitter. He was one man screaming at ten thousand people screaming at him. He berated and scolded his attackers and called them hypocrites. At first, all this made them even more incensed. But he didn't budge. He was a tireless defender of himself.

Eventually, it became clear to his critics that their fury was useless. They drifted away, until it all just stopped. And now, as Jonah Lehrer roamed the Los Angeles wilderness shattered and disgraced, Mike Daisey posted photographs on Instagram of him and his wife sunbathing poolside in Miami, having just completed a critically acclaimed sold-out theatrical tour. How could almost identical shamings annihilate one man and leave another without a scratch?

In the restaurant, Mike didn't reply to these questions right away. Then he said, "When I was young, twenty-one, twenty-two, my life fell apart in a really catastrophic way."

He had been staring down at the table. But now he looked up. "My girlfriend had suddenly started avoiding me," he continued. "I'd be, 'Let's get together.' But she always put me off. And finally I got a phone call. She was pregnant. Eight months pregnant. I was going to be a father. In a month."

This was in far northern Maine, Mike said. He felt trapped. In Maine. The baby was born. Their relationship disintegrated under the strain. "I abdicated my responsibilities as a father. I completely fell apart."

Every night Mike would go swimming in a lake. Some nights he swam out as far as he could. "I kept going. It got colder and colder. And I'd just lie in the lake. And I was trying, it's really clear now, I was trying to drown."

"You were trying to kill yourself?"

Mike nodded. "This is really clear to me now." He paused. "Ever since, I've never felt as tethered to this place as other people do. Everything seems like a long, improbable afterlife." Mike smiled. "I bring it up because it might be useful for you," he said.

We carried on eating. The story just hung there. I think Mike was treating me like an audience, feeding me fragments of stories, forcing me to piece together the mystery myself.

He swam back to shore each night. He ended up teaching high school drama. He graduated a year late. Then he left Maine. "I drove to Seattle," he said. "I tried to create a new life for myself." And he did. He became, of all things, a monologist in the theater. His shows were passionate and well liked but too esoteric to make a splash outside his fringe world. They were about esoteric things like how war had turned his grandfather cold and how that coldness had trickled down to turn his father cold. And so on. But then, in the summer of 2010, he performed his masterpiece—*The Agony and the Ecstasy of Steve Jobs*—the story of his trip to China.

The factory workers he met there told him about the n-hexane: "N-hexane is an iPhone screen cleaner," Mike's monologue went. "It's great because it evaporates a little bit faster than alcohol does, which means you can run the production line even faster and try to keep up with the quotas. The problem is that n-hexane is a potent neuro-toxin, and all these people have been exposed. Their hands shake uncontrollably. Most of them . . . can't even pick up a glass." His monologue moved on to describe his meetings with thirteen-year-old girls who worked at the plants because nobody checked ages, and the old man with the right hand that was "twisted up into a claw. It was crushed in a metal press at Foxconn." Mike showed this old man his iPad. "He's never actually seen one on, this thing that took his hand. I turn it on . . . the icons flare into view. And he strokes the screen with his ruined hand. And he says something . . . He says, 'It's a kind of magic.'"

One night at the end of 2011, *This American Life*'s creator, Ira Glass, saw Mike Daisey perform his show onstage at Joe's Pub in New York City. Like everyone else, he was spellbound, and so he offered Mike the chance to tell it on his program. The people at the show tried to fact-check. They asked Mike to put them in touch with his translator. But Mike said his phone number for her no longer worked. Some of his other facts had checked out, so they took his word for it.

I heard it go out live. I was driving through Florida. I pulled my car onto the side of the road and didn't move until it had finished. People all over America were doing the same. We felt inexorably altered by the power of Mike's narrative and became determined to take action. Most of us, it goes without saying, were inexorably altered back to how we'd been earlier that day by the time we'd had dinner or whatever.

But some weren't. One listener started a petition calling for better working conditions at Apple's manufacturing plants. He delivered 250,000 signatures. Pressure was put on the company like never before. It announced that, for the first time in its history, it would allow third parties in to audit the factory conditions. The Mike Daisey episode became the single most popular podcast in *This American Life*'s history.

But unbeknownst to Mike, his own Michael Moynihan was quietly digging.

He was Rob Schmitz, the Shanghai correspondent for the public radio show *Marketplace*. Some of Mike's details had seemed suspicious to him. For instance, Mike had mentioned interviewing factory workers in a Starbucks. How could they afford that? Starbucks is even more expensive in China than in the West. So he tracked down Mike's translator. And that's when Mike's story fell apart. There were no workers with hands that shook uncontrollably, no old man with a clawed hand. He hadn't visited "ten" plants in China. He'd visited three. And so on. It wasn't that the horrors Mike described hadn't happened—they had. One hundred thirty-seven workers at an Apple plant had been sickened by n-hexane, but it had happened in 2010 and a thousand miles away, in a town called Suzhou. (In Apple's February 2011 annual report, the company described the use of the toxic chemical as a "core violation" of worker safety and said it had ordered the contractor to stop using n-hexane.) Mike hadn't met these Suzhou workers. He'd only read about them. It just made his story more enthralling to pretend he was there.

And so, on March 16, 2012, Ira Glass brought Mike Daisey back on the air.

IRA GLASS: Were you afraid that we would discover something if we talked to [the translator]?

MIKE DAISEY: No, not really.

IRA: Really? There was no part of you which felt like, OK, well, the hexane thing didn't really happen when I was there. And did you feel like there was something that we would discover by talking to her?

MIKE: Well I did think it would unpack the complexities of, of like how, how the story gets told.

IRA: What does that mean, "unpack the complexities"?

MIKE: Well, it means that like the hexane thing, I think I'm agreeing with you. . . .

MIKE: I believe that when I perform it in a theatrical context . . . we have different languages for what the truth means.

IRA: I understand that you believe that, but I think you're kidding yourself. Normal people who go to see a person talk—people take it as a literal truth. I thought that the story was literally true seeing it in the theater. Brian, who's seen other shows of yours, thought all of them were true. . . .

MIKE: We have different worldviews on some of these things.

IRA: I know. But I feel like I have the normal worldview. The normal worldview is somebody stands onstage and says, "This happened to me," I think it happened to them, unless it's clearly labeled, "Here's a work of fiction." . . .

IRA: I have such a weird mix of feelings about this. Because I simultaneously feel terrible for you, and also, I feel lied to. And also, I stuck my neck out for you. I feel like I vouched for you. With our audience. Based on your word.

MIKE: I'm sorry.

The tone of voice in which Mike said, "I'm sorry," sounded like that of a child—a gifted, difficult, maverick child who thought he was bigger than the school—being made to stand in front of everyone and get chastened until he changed. In those three syllables he seemed to shift from defiant to broken.

But then he was back online, his self-esteem apparently totally revived.

He felt proud to have recovered the way he did. "I've been obsessed with investigating literary scandals," he told me. "Nobody ever comes back from those things. At the scale and intensity of what I experienced? Nobody comes out intact."

"I know!" I said. "Did you know from the start you'd survive?"

"Oh no," Mike said. "Oh no. I thought about killing myself."

I looked at him. "Really?" I said.

"Everything was on the table," he said. "I actively talked about killing myself. I actively talked about never performing again, just leaving the theater and never performing again. We talked about getting divorced. Very openly."

"How was your wife during this?" I said.

"She was making sure I wasn't alone," Mike said.

"When was all of this happening?" I asked.

"The very worst part of the scandal was before anyone knew of the scandal," he said. "There was a week between my interview with Ira and the show airing. During that week, I began to disassociate onstage. I was falling apart. I would freeze as I was doing the show. I would feel my mind take itself apart. That was the worst part. It was fucking terrible, the fear, and the feeling that you will dissolve."

"What were you most scared of?"

"I was terrified that I would no longer be able to tell the narrative of my life," Mike said, "that every time I performed onstage his judgment of me would echo forever, deciding who and what I was."

"So what changed?"

Mike didn't reply for a while. Then he said, "When Ira first asked me if I wanted to tell the story on his show, I thought, *This is a test. If I really believe in this, then the cowardly thing would be to not do the story. If I bury it, nothing will change.*" He paused. "I knew that the story would explode in the consciousness, and then it would explode for me."

I frowned. "You're saying you knew from the beginning that you'd be exposed?"

Mike nodded. "What happened on that lake showed me that there's a door," he said. "And the door is open a crack. And you can feel it. You can just die. You see? Once you accept that, it brings clarity. You want to do something in the world? Be willing to throw your life away. I was, 'Fine. I'll throw my life away. Fine.'"

"What about the risk that the scandal, instead of shining a

light on what was happening in China, would turn the light off?" I said.

"I would have worried about that a lot," Mike replied. Then he corrected his phrasing. "I worried about that a lot," he said. "I was really worried about that."

He could see me looking uncertainly at him.

"Look, nobody wants to hear that I am actually a heroic crusader and that I sacrificed myself," he said. "Nobody wants to hear that narrative. But that is, actually, the narrative. I knew there was no way it would withstand the scrutiny of becoming a major story. I knew it was going to fail."

I was sure I was watching a man in the process of building a fictional history for himself. In this new version of events, Mike had valiantly destroyed his reputation to save lives in China, like a suicide bomber. But at the time I felt I shouldn't tell him that I'd worked this out about him. It seemed to be what was holding him together.

But I think he read all this in my face, because he suddenly said: "The way we construct consciousness is to tell the story of ourselves to ourselves, the story of who we believe we are. I feel that a really public shaming or humiliation is a conflict between the person trying to write his own narrative and society trying to write a different narrative for the person. One story tries to overwrite the other. And so to survive you have to own your story. Or"—Mike looked at me—"you write a third story. You react to the narrative that's been forced upon you." He paused. "You have to find a way to disrespect the other narrative," he said. "If you believe it, it will crush you."

. . .

I was glad Mike Daisey had found a way to have a life. But I don't think his survival method was helpful advice for Jonah or Justine. They had no storytelling career to fall back on. There was no third narrative for them. There was just the one. Jonah was the fraudulent pop-science writer. Justine was the AIDS-tweet woman. They were tainted people and it wouldn't take a sleuth to find it out. Their flaws were right there on the front page of Google.

Justine made good on her promise. Five months after our first meeting we had lunch on Manhattan's Lower East Side. She filled me in on how her life had gone. She'd had a job offer right away, she said. But it was a weird one—from the owner of a Florida yachting company. "He said, 'I saw what happened to you. I'm fully on your side.'" But Justine knew nothing about yachts. So why did he want to hire her? "Was he a crazy person who thinks white people can't get AIDS?" She turned him down. Then she left New York. "In New York your career is your identity. I had that taken away from me." She went as far away as she could. To Addis Ababa, Ethiopia. She got a volunteer job with an NGO working to reduce maternal mortality rates.

"I thought that if I was going to be in this fucking terrible situation I should get something out of it, or at least try to make the most out of it and help people and learn." She flew there alone. "I knew where I was staying but there are no addresses. They don't really have street names. English is not their national language."

"Did you like it in Ethiopia?" I asked.

"It was fantastic," she said.

And this is where Justine's story could end. If you are one of the hundreds of thousands of people who tore her apart, you may want to make this your closing image of her. You may want to picture her in some makeshift maternity hospital in Addis Ababa. Perhaps she's bent over a woman in labor and she does something extraordinary to save the woman's life. Perhaps she glances up then, and wipes the desert sweat from her brow, and she's got a whole different facial expression—one of tough, proud wisdom or something. And it's all because of you. Justine would never have gone to Addis Ababa had she not been publicly shamed and fired from IAC.

But who was Justine kidding? Addis Ababa was great for a month, but she wasn't an Ethiopia person. She was a New York City person. She was nervy and sassy and sort of debonair. And so she came back. To a town where things were still not okay for her. She had temporary work doing the PR for the launch of a dating website, but she was not back on her feet. She was still fired from her dream job. She was still ridiculed and demonized across the Internet.

"I'm not fine yet," she said. "And I've really suffered."

She pushed the food around her plate. When I thought of Justine, I thought of a store looted in a riot. She may have left the door ajar, but she was all smashed up.

But I did notice one positive change in her. The first time

we'd met, she'd seemed ashamed—weighed down by the
guilt that she'd "tarnished" her family by pressing send on
that stupid tweet. I think she still felt ashamed, but maybe not
quite so much. Instead, she said, she felt humiliated.

The week I had lunch with Justine, the European Court
of Justice delivered an unexpected judgment—the Right to
Be Forgotten ruling. If an article or a blog about a person
was "inadequate, irrelevant or no longer relevant"—whatever
those vague words meant—Google must, if requested, de-
index it from its European sites (although not from Google
.com). Tens of thousands of people applied to be forgotten
straightaway—there'd be more than 70,000 applicants within
three months. Google complied vigorously, apparently as-
senting to practically every request. In fact, it complied so
vigorously—deindexing swaths of *Guardian* and *Daily Mail*
articles, for example, and then sending the newspapers automated notices informing them that they'd been deindexed—
the company seemed to be intentionally creating chaos to stir
up resistance to the judgment. Articles and websites sprung
up across the Internet attacking the ruling and outing the
forgotten: a football referee who had lied about his reasons
for giving a penalty, a couple arrested for having sex on a
train (who I'd forgotten all about until then), an airline,
Cathay Pacific, accused of racism by a Muslim job applicant.

Justine, following the news from New York, had "conflict-
ing feelings immediately," she told me. It seemed like censor-
ship to her. And it also seemed appealing. But she knew
invoking it would be a disaster for her. If the world found
out—imagine the frenzy. No. The Right to Be Forgotten
ruling would improve the life of some actual transgressor—

some barely shamed niche European former fraudster who slipped through the outers' net, for instance—far more than it would improve the life of the super-shamed Justine Sacco.

And so the worst thing, Justine said, the thing that made her feel most helpless, was her lack of control over the Google search results. They were just there, eternal, crushing.

"It's going to take a very long time for those Google search results to change for me," she said.

Eleven

The Man Who Can Change the Google Search Results

I n October 2012 a group of adults with learning difficulties took an organized trip to Washington, D.C. They visited the National Mall, the U.S. Holocaust Memorial Museum, the Smithsonian, Arlington National Cemetery, and the U.S. Mint. They saw the Tomb of the Unknown Soldier. At night they sang karaoke in the hotel bar. Their caregivers, Lindsey Stone and her friend Jamie, did a duet of "Total Eclipse of the Heart."

"They had the greatest time on that trip," Lindsey Stone told me. "We were laughing on the bus. We were laughing walking around at night. They thought that we were fun and cool."

Lindsey was telling me the story eighteen months later. We were sitting at her kitchen table. She lives down a long lane near a pretty lake in a seaside town on the East Coast of the United States. "I like to dance and I like to do karaoke," Lindsey said. "But for a long time after that trip I didn't leave the house. During the day, I'd just sit here. I didn't want to be seen by anybody. I didn't want people looking at me."

"How long did that last?" I asked her.

"Almost a year," she said.

Lindsey didn't want to talk to me about what had happened on that trip to Washington, D.C. I had written to her three times and she had ignored each of my letters. But a very peculiar circumstance had made it necessary for her to change her mind.

· · ·

L indsey and Jamie had been with LIFE—Living Independently Forever—for a year and a half before that trip. LIFE was a residence for "pretty high-functioning people with learning difficulties," Lindsey said. "Jamie had started a jewelry club, which was a hit with the girls. We'd take them to the movies. We'd take them bowling. We got the company to purchase a karaoke sound system. We heard a lot from parents that we were the best thing that ever happened to that campus."

Off duty, she and Jamie had a running joke—taking stupid photographs, "smoking in front of a NO SMOKING sign, or posing in front of statues, mimicking the pose. We took dumb pictures all the time. And so at Arlington we saw the SILENCE AND RESPECT sign. And inspiration struck."

"So," Lindsey said, "thinking we were funny, Jamie posted it on Facebook and tagged me on it with my consent because I thought it was hilarious."

Nothing much happened after that. A few Facebook friends posted unenthusiastic comments. "One of them had served in the military and he wrote a message saying, 'This is kind of offensive. I know you girls, but it's just tasteless.' Another said 'I agree' and another said 'I agree' and then I said, 'Whoa, whoa, whoa! It's just us being douchebags! Forget about it!'"

Whoa whoa whoa . . . wait. This is just us, being the douchebags that we are, challenging authority in general.

Much like the pic posted the night before, of me smoking right next to a no smoking sign. OBVIOUSLY we meant NO disrespect to people that serve or have served our country.

—LINDSEY STONE'S FACEBOOK MESSAGE, OCTOBER 20, 2012

After that, Jamie said to Lindsey, "Do you think we should take it down?"

"No!" Lindsey replied. "What's the big deal? No one's ever going to think of it again."

Their Facebook settings were a mystery to them. Most of the privacy boxes were ticked. Some weren't. Sometimes they'd half notice that boxes they'd thought they'd ticked weren't ticked. Lindsey has been thinking about that "a lot" these past eighteen months. "Facebook works best when everyone is sharing and liking. It brings their ad revenues up." Was there some Facebook shenanigan where things just "happen" to untick themselves? Some loophole? "But I don't want to sound like a conspiracy theorist. I don't know if Jamie's mobile uploads had ever been private."

Whatever: Jamie's mobile uploads weren't private. And four weeks after returning from Washington, D.C., they were in a restaurant celebrating their birthday—"We're a week apart"—when they became aware that their phones were vibrating repeatedly. So they went online.

"Lindsey Stone hates the military and hates soldiers who have died in foreign wars," and "Die cunt," and "You should rot in hell," and "Just pure Evil," and "The Face of a Typical Feminist. Fifty pounds overweight? Check. Sausage arms and

little piglet fingers? Check. No respect for the men who sacrificed? Check," and "Fuck You whore. I hope I die [sic] a slow
painful death. U retarted cunt," and "HOPE THIS CUNT
GETS RAPED AND STABBED TO DEATH," and "Spoke
with an employee from LIFE who has told me there are Veterans on the board and that she will be fired. Awaiting info
on her accomplice," and "After they fire her, maybe she needs
to sign up as a client. Woman needs help," and "Send the
dumb feminist to prison," and, in response to a small number
of posters suggesting that maybe a person's future shouldn't
be ruined because of a jokey photograph, "HER FUTURE
ISN'T RUINED! Stop trying to make her into a martyr. In
6 months no one except those that actually know her will
remember this."

"I wanted to scream, 'It was just about a sign,'" Lindsey
said.

Lindsey doesn't know how it spread. "I don't think I'll ever
know," she said. "We have a feeling that somebody at work
found it. We had kind of revitalized that campus. There was
animosity that came from that. They saw us as young, irrev-
erent idiots."

By the time she went to bed that night—"which was ad-
mittedly at four a.m."—a Fire Lindsey Stone Facebook page
had been created. It attracted 12,000 likes. Lindsey read every
comment. "I became really obsessed with reading everything
about myself."

The next day camera crews had gathered outside her front
door. Her father tried talking to them. He had a cigarette in
his hand. The family dog had followed him out. As he tried to
explain that Lindsey wasn't a terrible person, he noticed the

cameras move from his face down to the cigarette and the dog, like they were a family of hillbillies—smoking separatists down a lane with guard dogs.

LIFE was inundated with e-mails demanding their jobs, so Lindsey was called into work. But she wasn't allowed inside the building. Her boss met her in the parking lot and told her to hand over her keys.

"Literally, overnight everything I knew and loved was gone," Lindsey said.

And that's when she fell into a depression, became an insomniac, and barely left home for a year.

• • •

**COMPANY PRAISED FOR FIRING WOMAN
WHO TOOK DISRESPECTFUL PHOTO
NEXT TO SOLDIER'S GRAVE**

A company is being applauded for firing a woman who made a vulgar gesture next to a soldier's burial site, sparking nationwide outrage . . . Vitriol toward Lindsey Stone hasn't relented since she lost her job . . . Commentators suggested "she should be shot" or exiled from the United States . . .

Stone, who issued a statement of apology, has refused to show her face since the backlash, her parents told CBS Boston.

—RHEANA MURRAY, NEW YORK *Daily News*, NOVEMBER 22, 2012, AS SEEN ON PAGE ONE OF THE GOOGLE.COM RESULTS FOR THE SEARCH TERM "LINDSEY STONE"

During the year that followed the Washington, D.C., trip, Lindsey scanned Craigslist for caregiving work, but nobody ever replied to her applications. She lurked online, watching all the other Lindsey Stones get destroyed. "I felt so terrible for Justine Sacco," she said, "and that girl at Halloween who dressed like the Boston Marathon victim."

And then her life suddenly got much better. She was offered a job caring for children with autism.

"But I'm terrified," she said.

"That your bosses will find out?"

"Yeah."

Psychologists try to remind anxiety sufferers that "what if" worries are irrational ones. If you find yourself thinking, *What if I just came across as racist?* the "what if" is evidence that nothing bad *actually* happened. It's just thoughts swirling frantically around. But Lindsey's "what if" worry—"What if my new company googles me?"—was extremely plausible. In the tempest of her anxiety attacks there was no driftwood to hold on to. Her worst-case scenario was a *likely* one. And the photograph was everywhere. It had become so iconic and ubiquitous among swaths of U.S. veterans and right-wingers and antifeminists that one man had even turned it into patriotic wallpaper, superimposing onto the wall behind Lindsey's shrieking face and upturned finger a picture of a military funeral, complete with a coffin draped in the American flag.

Lindsey had wanted the job so much she'd been "nervous about even applying. And I wasn't sure how to address it on my résumé. Why the abrupt departure from LIFE? I was

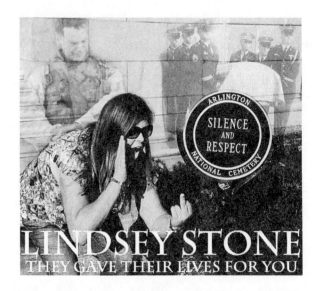

conflicted on whether to say to them, 'Just so you know, I am *this* Lindsey Stone.' Because I knew it was just a mouse click away."

Before the job interview, the question had haunted her. Should she tell them? She was "insanely nervous" about making the wrong decision. She left it until the moment of the interview. And then the interview was over and she found that she hadn't mentioned it.

"It just didn't feel right," she said. "People who have gotten to know me don't see Arlington as a big deal. And so I wanted to give them the opportunity to know me before I say to them, 'This is what you'll get if you google me.'"

She's been in the job four months, and she still hasn't told them.

"And obviously you can't ask them, 'Have you noticed it and decided it's not a problem?'" I said.

"Right," said Lindsey.

"So you feel trapped in a paranoid silence," I said.

"I love this job so much," Lindsey said. "I love these kids. One of the parents paid me a really high compliment the other day. I've only been working with her son for a month and she was like, 'The moment I met you, seeing the way you are with my son, and the way you treat people, you were meant to work in this field.' But I see everything with a heavy heart because I wait for the other shoe to drop. What if she found out? Would she feel the same way?" Lindsey could never just be happy and relaxed. The terror was always there. "It really impacts the way you view the world. Since it happened, I haven't tried to date anybody. How much do you let a new person into your life? Do they already know? The place I'm working at now—I was under the impression nobody knew. But someone made a comment the other day and I think they *knew*."

"What was the comment?"

"Oh, we were talking about something and he tossed off a comment like 'Oh, it's not like I'm going to plaster *that* all over the Internet.' Then he quickly said, 'Just kidding. I would never do that to somebody. I would never do that to you.'"

"So you don't know for *sure* that he knew."

"Exactly," Lindsey said. "But his hurried follow-up . . . I don't know." She paused. "That fear. It impacts you."

But now, suddenly, something had happened that could make all Lindsey's problems vanish. It was something almost magical, and it was my doing. I had set in motion a mysterious and fairy tale–like set of events for her. I'd never in my life been in a situation like this. It was new for both of us. It felt good—but there was a chance it wasn't good.

. . .

I t all started when I chanced upon the story of two former philosophy classmates from Harvard—Graeme Wood and Phineas Upham. There was something quite like Michael Moynihan and Jonah Lehrer about them. At Harvard—as Graeme Wood would later write—Phineas "dressed preppy and was a member of the Harvard chapter of the Ayn Rand cult. I wasn't poor, but no one in my family knew how heavy a bag with $300,000 in it felt."

What Graeme Wood meant was that in 2010—twelve years after leaving Harvard—Phineas Upham and his mother, Nancy, were arrested on tax-evasion charges. The indictment read that they conspired to hide $11 million in a Swiss bank account and then sneak the money in cash back to America. Graeme was intrigued by the news, so he set up a Google alert to "keep abreast of developments."

The scandal was over fast. Nancy pled guilty, was fined $5.5 million, and received a three-year suspended sentence. Soon after that, Graeme received a Google news alert about Phineas.

**U.S. DROPS CASE OF MAN ACCUSED
OF HELPING MOM HIDE MONEY**

The office of U.S. Attorney Preet Bharara in Manhattan has dropped an October 2010 indictment charging Sam-

uel Phineas Upham with one count of conspiracy to commit tax fraud and three counts of aiding in the preparation
of false tax returns . . . "The government has concluded
that further prosecution of the defendant would not be in
the interests of justice," prosecutors said in a May 18 filing
in federal court in New York.

—DAVID VOREACOS, *Bloomberg Businessweek*,
MAY 23, 2012

All charges against Phineas had been dropped. And so
that was that. Except Graeme never bothered to cancel his
Phineas Upham Google alert. Which was how he began to
notice the strange accolades. Phineas was suddenly garnering
a lot of them. He was appointed "Head Finance Curator of
Venture Cap Monthly," whatever that meant. "Charity News
Forum" voted him "Philanthropist of the Month." He started
writing for a magazine Graeme had never heard of called *Phi-
lanthropy Chronicle*. He published a collection of essays. He
even created a magazine to "bring philosophy writing to
underprivileged youth by making it part of nonprofit educational programs in developing nations."

But, as Graeme would write, "something was wrong with
these sites, which in every case looked flimsy and temporary,
especially when you got beyond the first page."

When I went to the street address listed for the [*Philan-
thropy Chronicle*] magazine's offices, I discovered that
64 Prince Street did not exist—or, rather, that it is a back
entrance next to an Indian restaurant.

What had begun as a schadenfreude-motivated Phineas Upham Google alert had led Graeme into the mysterious world of "black-ops reputation management." The purpose of the fake sites was obvious—to push reports about the tax-evasion charges so far down the search results that they'd effectively vanish. Nobody had heard of the European Court of Justice's "Right to Be Forgotten" ruling at that point—it was still two years from existing—but somebody was evidently fashioning some clumsy homemade U.S.-based version for Phineas Upham.

Graeme had a skill most people don't. He knew how to attain clues from HTML codes. So he dug into them, "looking for evidence of a common author." And he found it. The fake sites were the work of a man named Bryce Tom, the head of a business called Metal Rabbit Media. He was a young Californian living in New York City.

The two men met in a café, Graeme thrilled to have exposed the mother lode, Bryce Tom evidently plagued with anxiety.

"This could be very bad for me," he said, visibly shaken. "No one's going to want my business." We stared at each other in uneasy silence for a few minutes, and I fetched him a nonalcoholic sangria to calm him down. When I returned, Tom had shredded his napkin.

—Graeme Wood, "Scrubbed,"
New York magazine, June 16, 2013

I found Graeme's story strange and enthralling except for this last part. Bryce Tom had seemed in such despair that he'd been exposed, which made for a melancholy ending.

And now Graeme and I sat opposite each other in a New York City café. I told him I hadn't a clue that people like Bryce Tom existed and I wanted to do some digging of my own. Graeme gave me leads: names of men and women he suspected might be Metal Rabbit clients, like a highly decorated UN peacekeeper who had twice been blown up in suicide bombings. Back home, I read articles about how, on both occasions, bleeding from shrapnel wounds, this UN peacekeeper stayed to help the wounded and the dying. The stories were full of eulogies, tributes to his bravery, "but his Wikipedia page has been edited by a man I know works for Metal Rabbit," Graeme had told me. And after an hour of hacking through Google's undergrowth, I found a site accusing the peacekeeper of being a philanderer, cheating on three women at the same time, a "low life prick," and a "pathological liar [whose] behavior is demonic." When I e-mailed him to ask if he was a Metal Rabbit client, he obliquely replied that he wasn't but "I do know the guys."

Like Graeme Wood, I was having fun exploring the Google search pages nobody ever goes to for secrets that would otherwise go unnoticed, but then I met Justine and heard about Lindsey, and I read Graeme's article a second time and saw a different side to it. It was miserable that 99 percent of us could never afford a service like Metal Rabbit, and it was intriguing and scandalous that people like Bryce Tom went about their business in such a shadowy manner. Metal Rabbit deserved exposure. But Phineas Upham had been cleared of all charges. Surely he had a right to be forgotten? Didn't he?

I e-mailed Bryce Tom, "Is Metal Rabbit Media still operational?"

He e-mailed back, "What can I help you with?"

I e-mailed him back, "I'm a journalist . . ."

I never heard from him again.

. . .

The Village Pub in Woodside, near Menlo Park, Silicon Valley, looks like no big deal from the outside, but when you get inside, you realize it's massively upmarket and filled with tech billionaires—the restaurant version of the non-threatening clothes the tech billionaires were wearing. I told my dining companion, Michael Fertik, that he was the only person from the mysterious reputation-management world who had returned my e-mail.

"That's because this is a really easy sector in which to be an unappealing, scurrilous operation," he said.

"Scurrilous in what way?"

"A couple of them are really nasty fucking people," Michael said. "There's a guy who has some traction in our space, who runs a company, he's a convicted rapist. He's a *felony rapist*. He went to jail for four years for raping a woman. He started a company to basically obscure that fact about himself, I think." Michael told me the name of the man's company. "We've built a data file on him," he said.

Michael's competitors were disreputable, he said, and so were some of his potential clients.

"Very early on, within two weeks of launching our website in 2006 [Michael's company is called Reputation.com] I remember being by myself and getting a couple of sign-ups from guys. So I googled them. They were pedophiles."

"Do you remember the pedophiles' names?" I asked Michael.

"Of course not," Michael said. "Why do you ask that shit?"

"I don't know," I said. "Curiosity."

"No, it's prurient curiosity of the type you condemn in your book," Michael said.

Michael looked different from our fellow diners. I didn't recognize any of them, but everyone seemed insanely rich—preppy, with faces like luxury yachts, like Martha's Vineyard in the summertime, WASPy and at peace with the world, practically floating through the restaurant, whereas Michael was a big, angry, coiled-spring Jewish bear of a man. He was born in New York City, attained a degree from Harvard Law School, and invented the concept of online reputation management while working as a clerk for the Sixth Circuit of the U.S. Court of Appeals in Louisville, Kentucky. This was the mid-2000s. Stories about cyberbullying and revenge porn were just starting to filter through. And that's how Michael got the idea.

After he turned the pedophiles down, Michael told me, he noticed he was getting sign-ups from neo-Nazis, albeit repentant former ones—*"When I was seventeen I was a Nazi. I was an asshole kid. Now I'm in my 40s I'm trying to move on but the Internet still thinks that I am a Nazi."* They were more sympathetic than the pedophiles, but Michael, being Jewish, still didn't want them as clients. So he drew up a code of conduct. He wouldn't accept anyone who was under investigation or had been convicted of a felony violent crime, or a felony fraud crime, or any sexually violent crime, or anyone accused—even informally—of a sexual crime against children. And, he said, there was another moral difference between him and his competitors. He wouldn't invent fake accolades. He'd only put the truth up there. Although "I don't think it's incumbent on anyone to do massive fact-checking."

"I have no idea what you actually do," I had told Michael over the telephone before our dinner. "I don't know how you manipulate Google search results."

I understood that Michael was offering some kind of stealthier version of the European Court of Justice's Right to Be Forgotten ruling. Plus, unlike the ruling, Michael had a worldwide reach, not just a European one. As it happened, the judgment wasn't working out well for a lot of its applicants. They were finding themselves less forgotten than ever, given that so many journalists and bloggers had dedicated themselves to outing them. But nobody was scrutinizing the client lists of the online reputation management companies.

Only a few very unlucky people, like Phineas Upham, had been exposed that way.

"Your work is a total mystery to me," I said to Michael. "Especially the technological side of it. Maybe I could follow someone through the process?"

"Sure," Michael replied.

And so we planned it out. We'd just need to find a willing client. Which wouldn't be easy given that my pitch was that I wanted to study something they were frantically attempting to conceal. It was not a winning pitch.

We talked about generic possibilities. Maybe I could convince a victim of "revenge porn," Michael suggested, some woman whose spurned boyfriend had posted naked photographs of her online. Or maybe I could convince a politician who had said some offhand thing and wanted it buried before it devoured him. Or, oh, Michael added, somewhat less generically, maybe I could convince the leader of a religious group who was currently being falsely accused online of murdering his brother.

I coughed. "How about the leader of the religious group being falsely accused of murdering his brother?" I said.

I'll call the religious leader Gregory. Which is not his real name. Plus, I've changed some details of his story to make him unidentifiable for reasons that will become obvious. Gregory's brother—a member of Gregory's religious group— had been found dead in a hotel room. A member of Gregory's flock had been arrested for the murder. The investigating officers had apparently discounted Gregory as a co-conspirator.

But message boards were ablaze with speculation that he'd directed it as if he were some kind of Charles Manson.

Which was where Reputation.com had come in. Gregory hadn't approached them. Their outreach team had noticed the accusations and had pitched him their services. I don't know how far that conversation had gone. But now Michael talked to Gregory about taking him on as a client pro bono on the condition that I would be allowed to witness it all.

Gregory e-mailed me. He was appreciative of Michael's offer, he wrote, and might consent to an interview with me—his tone made "consent to an interview" sound like "deign to consent to an interview," I thought—but he was puzzled. Given that my previous books were about such frivolous topics as military psychics and conspiracy theorists, why did I suppose my readers would be interested in the important subject of public shaming?

Oh, my God, I thought. *He's right.*

Gregory added that he was sorry if he was offending me, but why did I presume that my views on the serious subject of public shaming would be taken seriously by anyone, given that my previous books sounded so implausible?

That IS a bit offensive, I thought.

Gregory seemed suspicious that the murder-mystery aspect of his story was more captivating to me than the public shaming part. And what could I say? He was right. I was happy to have Gregory's name purged from the Internet if I could get to hear the intriguing details. I was the Selfish Giant, wanting to keep the lavish garden for myself and my readers, while building a tall wall around it so nobody else could look in.

Gregory and I e-mailed back and forth about thirty times during the days that followed. My e-mails were breezy. Gregory's e-mails alluded darkly to "conditions." I ignored the word "conditions" and carried on being breezy. Finally, Gregory wrote that the good news was that he'd decided to grant me an exclusive interview, so he was instructing his lawyer to draw up a contract in which I agreed to portray him in a positive way or else suffer significant financial penalty.

And that was the end of my relationship with Gregory.

Now that I no longer needed to be on my best behavior in my e-mails to him, I let it all out. "For about a thousand reasons there is no way on Earth I would sign a contract promising to be positive or risk significant financial penalty," I e-mailed. "I've never heard of such a thing! I can't tell you how frowned upon something like that is in journalism. NO ONE does it. If I signed that, you could determine anything negative and take my money! What if, God forbid, you get charged? What if we have a falling out?"

Gregory wished me the best of luck with my book.

It was frustrating. Michael Fertik was offering free services to a shamed person of my choice and I was finding it difficult to provide him with one who wasn't unpleasantly overbearing. The fact was, even though Gregory hadn't been charged with any crime, his weird and controlling e-mails had made me feel warier of the online reputation management world. What other cracks were being papered over?

Michael had accused me of "prurient curiosity of the type you condemn in your book" when I'd asked him about the early pedophile sign-ups he'd thwarted. And now the accusation put me in a panic. I didn't want to write a book that advocated for a less curious world. Prurient curiosity may not be great. But curiosity is. People's flaws need to be written about. The flaws of some people lead to horrors inflicted on others. And then there are the more human flaws that, when you shine a light onto them, de-demonize people who might otherwise be seen as ogres.

But there was a side of Michael's business I respected—the side that offered salvation to people who'd really done nothing wrong but had been dramatically shamed anyway. Like Justine Sacco. Which is why I now e-mailed Michael's publicist, Leslie Hobbs, suggesting Justine as Gregory's replacement: "I think she's a deserving case," I wrote. "She may not go for it. But should I at least put it to her as a possibility?"

Leslie didn't reply to my e-mail. I sent another one asking why they didn't want to consider taking Justine on. She didn't reply to that one either. I took the hint. I didn't want to lose their goodwill, so I threw Justine on the fire and came up with a new name—a public shamee I'd written to three times and had heard nothing back. Lindsey Stone.

It was the first time I'd ever been in a position to offer an incentive to a reluctant interviewee. I'd witnessed other journalists do it and had always glared at them with hatred from across the room. Twenty years ago I covered the rape trial of a British TV presenter. Journalists on the press bench were shooting him likable little smiles in the hope of an exclusive interview should he be found not guilty. It was embarrassing. And futile too: On the day of his acquittal a woman in a fur coat appeared in court from nowhere and whisked him away. It turned out that she was from the *News of the World.* All the other journalists—with their likable little smiles—had never stood a chance. This woman had a checkbook.

I still had no checkbook, but without Michael's inducement, I'd have had no chance with Lindsey. And it was quite the inducement.

"We'll end up spending hundreds of thousands of bucks on her," Michael said. "At least a hundred grand. Up to several hundred grand of effort."

"Hundreds of thousands?" I said.

"Her situation is very dire," he said.

"Why does it cost so much?" I asked him.

"Take it up with Google." He shrugged. "It sucks to be Lindsey Stone."

I thought Michael was being unbelievably generous.

I didn't tell Lindsey that she nearly lost out to Justine Sacco and the leader of a religious group who had been falsely accused of murdering his brother. Gregory's story had overbeguiled me. But Lindsey was perfect. With her, there were no strange caveats, no domineering e-mails. All she wanted was to work with autistic children and not feel the terror.

"If Michael takes you on, that photograph might practically vanish," I said to her.

"That would be unbelievable," she replied. "Or if it just

disappeared two pages down Google. Only creepy people check past the second page."

Lindsey knew it wasn't perfect. My book would inevitably bring it back up again. But she understood that anything would be better than the way things were now. She was being offered hundreds of thousands of dollars in free services. This was bespoke—a shaming-eradication service that only the superrich could normally afford. After I left Lindsey's house, she and Michael talked on the phone. After that, Michael called me.

"She was nothing but very gracious and responsive and cooperative," he said. "I think we can proceed."

. . .

For scheduling reasons, Michael couldn't start on Lindsey for a few months, and so I took a break. I've worked on dark stories before—stories about innocent people losing their lives to the FBI, about banks hounding debtors until they commit suicide—but although I felt sorry for those people, I hadn't felt the dread snake its way into me in the way these shaming stories had. I'd leave Jonah and Michael and Justine feeling nervous and depressed. And so it was a nice surprise to receive an e-mail from Richard Branson's sister Vanessa inviting me to appear at a salon of talks at her Marrakech palace/holiday home/hotel, the Riad El Fenn. "Other speakers," she e-mailed, "include Clive Stafford Smith—human-rights lawyer. David Chipperfield—architect. Hans-Ulrich Obrist—Serpentine curator. Redha Moali—

rags-to-riches Algerian arts entrepreneur." I googled her Riad. It combines "grandeur and historic architecture with hideaway nooks, terraces and gardens" and is "just five minutes walk from the world-famous Djemaa el Fna square and bustling maze of streets that make up the souk."

And so it was that, four weeks later, I sat reading a book underneath an orange tree in Vanessa Branson's Marrakech courtyard. Vanessa Branson lay supine on a velvet bed in the corner. Her friends lounged around, drinking herbal teas. One had been the CEO of Sony in Germany, another owned a diamond mine in South Africa. I was feeling tired and jittery and less languid than the others, who were dressed in white linen and seemed carefree.

Then I heard a noise. I looked up from my book. Vanessa Branson was rushing across the courtyard to welcome someone new. He too was dressed in linen and was tall and thin, with the gait of a British man of privilege. He might have been a diplomat. After a few minutes, he bounded over to me. "I'm Clive Stafford Smith," he said.

I knew a little about him from his interview on BBC Radio 4's *Desert Island Discs*—how he was all set for a life in British society until one day at his boarding school he saw a drawing in a book of Joan of Arc being burned at the stake and realized she looked like his sister. So in his twenties he became a death-row lawyer in Mississippi, and he has been defending death-row and Guantánamo prisoners ever since. The *Desert Island Discs* presenter, Sue Lawley, treated him with baffled amazement, like Queen Victoria would a lord who had gone off to explore darkest Africa. Ten minutes after introducing himself, he was walking me through the corridors of Vanessa Branson's labyrinthine palace telling me why prisons should be abolished.

"Let me ask you three questions," he said. "And then you'll see it my way. Question One: What's the worst thing that you have ever done to someone? It's okay. You don't have to confess it out loud. Question Two: What's the worst criminal act that has ever been committed against you? Question Three: Which of the two was the most damaging for the victim?"

The worst criminal act that has ever been committed against me was burglary. How damaging was it? Hardly damaging at all. I felt theoretically violated at the idea of a stranger wandering through my house. But I got the insurance money. I was mugged one time. I was eighteen. The man who mugged me was an alcoholic. He saw me coming out of a supermarket. "Give me your alcohol," he yelled. He punched me in the face, grabbed my groceries, and ran away. There wasn't any alcohol in my bag. I was upset for a few weeks, but it passed.

And what was the worst thing I had ever done to someone? It was a terrible thing. It was devastating for them. It wasn't against the law.

Clive's point was that the criminal justice system is supposed to repair harm, but most prisoners—young, black—have been incarcerated for acts far less emotionally damaging than the injuries we noncriminals perpetrate upon one another all the time—bad husbands, bad wives, ruthless bosses, bullies, bankers.

I thought about Justine Sacco. How many of the people

piling on her had been emotionally damaged by what they had read? As far as I could tell, only one person was damaged in that pile-on.

"I'm writing a book about public shaming," I told Clive. "With citizen justice, we're bringing public shame back in a big way. You've spent your life in actual courts. Is it the same there? Is shaming utilized as a kind of default position in real courtrooms too?"

"Oh, yes!" he replied, quite happily. "I do it all the time. I've humiliated a lot of people. Especially experts."

"What's your method?" I asked him.

"Oh, it's a very simple game," he said. "You need to figure out something that's so esoteric the expert can't possibly know about it. Maybe it's something that's not relevant to the case, but it has to be something they cannot know the answer to. They'll be incapable of saying they don't know. So they'll gradually walk down the garden to the place where they look really stupid."

"Why are they incapable of saying they don't know?"

"It's their entire profession," Clive said. "It's respect. It's a big deal being an expert. Imagine the things you can discuss at dinner parties as opposed to the other boring people at the table. You're the witness who put Ted Bundy away. They'll do anything to not look stupid. That's the key thing. And if you can make them look stupid, everything else falls by the wayside."

Clive made it sound as if shaming were as natural as breathing in the court world and as if it had been that way forever. And, of course, I understood that witnesses needed to be grilled, their honesty tested. But it's odd that so many of us see shaming how free-market libertarians see capitalism, as a beautiful beast that must be allowed to run free.

Those of us on social media were just starting out on our shaming crusade. In the real courts, according to Clive, it was venerated as a first-line tactic. I wondered: When shaming takes on a disproportionate significance within an august institution, when it entrenches itself over generations, what are the consequences? What does it do to the participants?

Twelve

The Terror

A dozen men and women sat around a conference table at the Piccadilly Hotel in Manchester. There was a marine metallurgist, a pediatric nurse, an occupational therapist specializing in brain injuries, a laboratory technician working with the metropolitan police drug squad, someone from the tobacco industry, a social worker who visits the homes of parents suspected of abusing or neglecting their children, and so on. These people had just one thing in common: They were rookie court expert witnesses. They were all hoping to make extra money from the court world. Like me, they didn't know the minutiae of how a day in court worked. None of them had yet been called as experts. Which was why they had signed up for this "courtroom familiarization" course, organized by the legal-training company Bond Solon. I had signed up after my conversation with Clive. I was curious to know if shaming was a significant enough part of the court milieu to merit a mention in a courtroom familiarization course.

It merited a mention straightaway. There was a whiteboard. Our trainer for the day, John, stood next to it. "You," he told us, by way of introduction, "are a bone being dragged over by two dogs that want to win. And if you get between the lawyer and his goal, you're going to get hurt." He surveyed the room. "Appreciate what the lawyer is trying to do. The lawyer hopes to drag you down. He'll call you incompetent, inexperienced. You might start to feel angry, upset. He will try and drag you outside your area of expertise, your circle of facts. How? How will he try to do this?"

There was a silence. Then it dawned on the rookie experts that this wasn't a rhetorical question.

"Facial expression?" the marine metallurgist said.

"What do you mean?" said John.

"Smiling or not smiling," the metallurgist said. "Looking unmoved. Lulling us into a false sense of security and then pouncing. Looking bored?"

John wrote the suggestions down on the whiteboard.

"Unnerve us with a disbelieving, patronizing, or sarcastic voice?" asked the social worker.

"Might they snigger?" the lab technician asked.

"No, that would sound unprofessional," said John. "But they might go for incredulity. They might say, 'Really?'"

"What would happen if I nervously laugh?" the lab technician said. "Sometimes, when I'm under pressure, I nervously laugh."

"Don't," John warned. "If you do, they'll say, 'Are you finding it *funny*? My *client* isn't.'"

"Are we allowed to ask them to stop if it gets too much for us?" the marine metallurgist said.

"No," said John. "You aren't allowed to ask them to stop. Any other guesses?"

"Pretend to mispronounce your name?" someone said.

"Silence?" someone else said. Everyone cringed at the thought of silence.

"Should we be concerned about the color of our clothes?" asked a care worker. "I hear someone wearing brown is considered less believable."

"That's too deep for me," said John.

I assumed that by lunchtime John would move away from shaming familiarization to other types of courtroom familiarization. But, really, that never happened. It turned out that shaming was such an integral part of the judicial process that the day was pretty much *all* about it. In the afternoon the experts were taught shame-avoidance techniques. When they first enter the dock, John told them, they should ask the court usher to bring them a glass of water. That would give them a moment to settle their nerves. They mustn't pour the water themselves, but instead ask the court usher to. When the lawyer asks them a question, they should swivel on their hips and deliver their answer to the judge.

"They'll have a much harder time breaking you down that way," John said. "Oddly enough, we like to look at our tormentors. Maybe it's linked into the Stockholm syndrome."

The day ended with a mock cross-examination—a chance for the rookie experts to enact what they had learned. Matthew the marine metallurgist was the first to take the fake witness stand. John asked me to pretend to be the judge. Everyone smiled supportively at Matthew. He was a young man, wearing a pink shirt and a pink tie. He was shaking a little. He poured himself a glass of water. The water in the glass shook like a pond during a minor tremor.

He forgot to ask the usher to pour him a glass of water, I thought.

"Tell me your qualifications," said John, taking the role of the cross-examining lawyer.

"I have an upper first-class degree, sorry, second-class degree in metallurgy," said Matthew, looking John in the eye.

Then he bowed his head, like a geisha.

Why is he not turning to face me? I thought.

Matthew's role-play lasted fifteen minutes. His face turned as crimson as a rusted cargo container as he mumbled about corroded coils. His mouth was dry, his voice trembling. He was a wreck.

He's weak, I felt myself think. *He's just so weak.*

Then I caught myself. Judging someone on how flustered he behaves in the face of a shaming is a truly strange and arbitrary way of forming an opinion on him.

• • •

started corresponding with a woman from the Scottish town of New Cumnock. Her name was Linda Armstrong. One September night Linda's sixteen-year-old daughter, Lindsay, was on her way home from a nearby bowling alley when a fourteen-year-old boy from the town followed her off the bus, coaxed her into a park, pushed her to the ground, and raped her. At the boy's trial Lindsay was cross-examined by his lawyer, John Carruthers. Linda sent me a copy of the court transcript. "I have never read it," she wrote to me, "because I couldn't face it."

LINDSAY ARMSTRONG: He started following behind me and he was asking me out and everything and I kept saying no and then I walked away from him and then he followed behind me and he pulled my arm like that and he started trying to kiss me and everything and I kept shoving him away. I told him to leave me alone and then he shoved me down . . .

JOHN CARRUTHERS: I wonder if we could see label number 7 please. Do you recognize those?

LINDSAY ARMSTRONG: Uh huh.

JOHN CARRUTHERS: What are they?

LINDSAY ARMSTRONG: My pants.

JOHN CARRUTHERS: Those are the pants that you were wearing that day?

LINDSAY ARMSTRONG: Uh huh.

JOHN CARRUTHERS: I wonder if you could hold them up to allow people to see them. Would it be fair to describe those pants as flimsy?

LINDSAY ARMSTRONG: I don't think what kind of pants I wear has anything to do with . . .

JOHN CARRUTHERS: Well, hold them up again. It has got a name, the design of it, hasn't it? What's it called? Is it not a thong?

LINDSAY ARMSTRONG: Yes.

JOHN CARRUTHERS: I beg your pardon, Miss Armstrong. If I could ask you to hold them up?

LINDSAY ARMSTRONG: Sorry.

JOHN CARRUTHERS: Now you can see through those pants, is that correct?

LINDSAY ARMSTRONG: Uh huh.

JOHN CARRUTHERS: What does it say on the front?

LINDSAY ARMSTRONG: Little devil.

JOHN CARRUTHERS: Sorry?

LINDSAY ARMSTRONG: Little devil.

"Lindsay told me she was disgusted and very embarrassed about him making her hold up her underwear," Linda e-mailed me. "She said she put them back down quickly and he shouted at her to pick them up again. Purely to let the jury see what type of underwear she wore. I think this was probably the most stressful part of the cross-examination for her, as she didn't ever want to see those clothes again. There was absolutely no need for her to read out what was written on the front of them."

The boy was found guilty. He was sentenced to four years

in a young-offenders' institution (he eventually served two). Three weeks after the cross-examination, Lindsay's parents found her in her bedroom at two a.m. She had put on "Bohemian Rhapsody" and had taken a lethal overdose of antidepressants.

A shaming can be like a distorting mirror at a funfair, taking human nature and making it look monstrous. Of course, it was tactics like those John Carruthers had used that compelled us to believe we could do justice better on social media. But still: Knee-jerk shaming is knee-jerk shaming and I wondered what would happen if we made a point of eschewing the shaming completely—if we refused to shame anyone. Could there be a corner of the justice system trying out an idea like that? It turned out that there was. And it was being run by about the last person you'd expect.

Thirteen

Raquel in a
Post-Shaming
World

A little boy and his father were eating breakfast at an almost deserted restaurant in the Meatpacking District of Manhattan when they became aware of a man dashing across the floor toward them. He seemed to have something urgent to say. The boy looked anxious at what might happen next. The stranger took a breath.

"STUDY HARD AT MATH!" he yelled.

There was a silence. "Okay," the boy said.

At this, the man walked over to me and sat down, pleased to have had the chance to positively motivate a child. His phone rang. "Sorry," he mouthed. He picked it up. "DID YOU DO TEN STRONG POWERFULS LAST NIGHT?" he hollered at the receiver. "WORD OF HONOR? GOOD FOR YOU! LOVE YOU, BYE!" He put the phone down. Then he smiled, delighted that this was proving to be such a gold-rush morning for him in terms of imparting inspirational messages.

His name was Jim McGreevey. He used to be the governor of New Jersey. He'd been a severe one too: "I never pardoned anyone," he told me.

"How does the pardoning process even work?" I asked him.

"The attorney general's office makes a recommendation," he replied. "They contact the local county prosecutor, who contacts the parole officer of the person being considered for a pardon, who makes an official recommendation to the governor. Who was me."

I pictured the prisoners in their cells, concentrating hard on their letters to Jim, frantically wondering how best to lay out their mitigating circumstances. What would draw Jim in? What would grab the attention of the governor?

"Can you remember any of their stories?" I asked Jim.

"I never read any of them," he said.

"You never even *looked*?"

Jim shook his head.

"You were like a hanging judge," I said.

"I was a law-and-order Democrat," Jim said.

• • •

Bill and Hillary Clinton had campaigned for Jim back in
2001. He was young, handsome, and married, with two
beautiful daughters. He won a landslide victory and took
his place at the heart of the New Jersey power elite—"as
close," as he'd later describe the state in his memoirs, "to
Machiavelli's cutthroat Venetian principality as anywhere
on Earth." It was a place where "political meetings start with
a big bear hug" so that each hugger could surreptitiously
check the other for a concealed wire: "A New Jersey pat
down among friends." Now Jim had a beach house, a heli-
copter, a staff of cooks, and Drumthwacket, the governor's
mansion.

Jim considered himself awesome. He was inviolable. This

Drumthwacket

was just after 9/11. He'd turn up at places like the offices of the Bergen *Record*—North Jersey's regional newspaper— and hold forth, lording over the journalists, making grand pronouncements like "We will not skimp on security. We've even employed a security adviser from the Israeli Defense Forces, probably the best in the world." Then he'd swan off, thinking how well it had gone, unaware that the editorial board of the Bergen *Record* was now wondering why on earth the governor of New Jersey had employed a man from the Israeli Defense Forces to advise on local security.

• • •

When Jim was a young boy, he'd lie in his tent at summer camp and "think I was hearing people in other tents call me a faggot and then realize that they were." Jim stirred his coffee. "It's funny how these things just stay."

"They really stay," I said. "My life at fifteen and sixteen never leaves me."

We looked at each other then—Jim and I—two middle-aged men in a coffee shop in New York City.

Jim grew up, went to Columbia University, and would some nights walk all the way down from 116th Street to the Meat-packing District to look into the windows of the gay bars. But he couldn't bring himself to go inside and he'd walk back up to 116th Street.

He grew up to become an assistant prosecutor—"a prosecutor's prosecutor"—and a town mayor. He read books on how to stop having gay thoughts. As a state assemblyman, he voted against gay marriage.

He lost his first election campaign for the governorship by just twenty-seven thousand votes (out of more than two million votes cast). When he was campaigning for the second time, he went on a diplomatic junket to Israel where he found himself at a lunch in some rural town. The man sitting next to him introduced himself. His name was Golan, he said, and he worked for the local mayor.

"I followed your campaign very closely," Golan told Jim. "Twenty-seven thousand votes is a very narrow margin."

Jim was, he'd later write, "flattered beyond anything I'd ever experienced before. Nobody commits to memory the demographic standings of a politician halfway around the world."

Jim fell in love with Golan. He told him that if he came to New Jersey he'd give him an important concocted job title like "special counselor to the governor." Golan agreed and, on his arrival in America, demanded an especially opulent office that had already been allocated to another member of Jim's staff. Jim gave Golan the office.

. . .

A few weeks after Jim's visit to the Bergen *Record*, the newspaper published a profile of the unexpected Israeli staff member, referring to Golan as a "sailor" (he had once been in the Israeli navy) and a "poet" (he'd written a collection of poems in high school). Jim feared they might be using code words, but he didn't know for sure and he couldn't talk to anyone about it. His staff was acting like nothing was different, but that didn't mean nothing was different.

"People don't say things to governors that they don't think governors want to hear," he told me.

Jim distanced himself from Golan. He told him he needed to quit his job for the good of the administration. Golan was devastated. He had envisaged a great career in U.S. politics and now Jim was throwing him on the fire to save his own career.

A few weeks later, a letter arrived for Jim. It was from Golan's lawyer. Golan was threatening to sue Jim for sexual assault and harassment.

"When I got that letter, I had this vision of my grandmother's china cabinet," Jim told me. "And all the china was just smashing."

After three years in power, it was over for Jim. He called a press conference. "I am a gay American," he announced.

He confessed the affair, resigned the governorship, stepped off the stage, checked himself into the Meadows, an Arizona clinic, and was diagnosed with posttraumatic stress disorder.

•   •   •

You *met* James Gilligan?" Jim said to me in the restaurant. "Oh, I *love* Gilligan. I love Gilligan."

In fact, I had met James Gilligan at the very beginning of

my journey—a few days after Jonah Lehrer had made his disastrous apology speech at the Knight Foundation lunch. Gilligan is in late middle age now, with the worried face and wispy hair and wire-rimmed glasses of the East Coast psychiatrist he is. I sat with him in the communal courtyard of his apartment in New York City's West Village. He's about the world's best-informed chronicler of what a shaming can do to our inner lives, which is why he's so opposed to its renaissance on social media. I wanted to learn how he came to make it his life's work.

Back in the 1970s, Gilligan told me, he was a young psychiatrist at Harvard Medical School. His days were spent "treating middle-class neurotics like you and me." He was completely uninterested in the strange epidemic that was occurring within Massachusetts's prisons and mental hospitals "of suicides and homicides and riots and hostage taking and fire setting and everything you can imagine that was dangerous. Prisoners were getting killed, officers were getting killed, visitors were getting killed. It was completely out of control during the entire decade of the 1970s. There was a murder a month in one prison alone, and a suicide every six weeks."

Inmates were swallowing razor blades and blinding and castrating themselves and each other. A U.S. District Court judge, W. Arthur Garrity, ordered the Department of Corrections to make sense of the chaos by bringing in a team of investigative psychiatrists. Gilligan was invited to lead the group. He agreed, but he wasn't enthusiastic. He assumed the perpetrators of the prison violence would be psychopaths.

"I'd been taught that psychopaths had just been born that way," he said, "and that they'd only want to manipulate you so you'd get them a reduced sentence."

He pictured them like they were another species. And that's exactly how they seemed to him when he first went inside the Bridgewater State Hospital for the criminally insane.

"One of the first men I met had been a pimp in a slum area of Boston," Gilligan said. "He killed some of his girls, and he killed other people. He killed several people in the community before he was finally arrested. So they put him in the Charles Street jail to await trial. And he promptly killed one of the inmates there. So they said, 'He's too violent to await trial in the jail. We have to send him to Walpole'—the maximum-security prison. And he killed someone *there*. And that's when I met him. He looked like a zombie. He was mute, rather paranoid, not overtly psychotic but literally abnormal. Everybody was scared to death of him. I thought, *This guy's untreatable*. But we needed to keep people safe. So we put him in a locked dormitory building, and during the day, I told the staff, 'Keep an invisible wall around him. Keep six feet away from him. Don't crowd him. If you crowd him, you might get injured.'"

And that's how things remained for a while. But eventually the man—and other men like him—loosened up a little to Gilligan. And what they told him came as a great surprise to him.

"The men would all say that they had died," Gilligan said. "These were the most incorrigibly violent characters. They would all say that they themselves had died before they started killing other people. What they meant was that their personalities had died. They felt dead inside. They had no capacity for feelings. No emotional feelings. Or even physical feelings. So some would cut themselves. Or they would mutilate themselves in the most horrible ways. Not because they felt guilty—this wasn't a penance for their sins—but because they wanted to see if they *had* feelings. They found their inner numbness more tormenting than even the physical pain would be."

Gilligan filled notepads with observations from his interviews with the men. He wrote, "Some have told me that they feel like robots or zombies, that their bodies are empty or filled with straw, not flesh and blood, that instead of having veins and nerves they have ropes or cords. One inmate told me he feels like 'food that is decomposing.' These men's souls did not just die. They have dead souls because their souls were murdered. How did it happen? How were they murdered?"

This was, Gilligan felt, the mystery he'd been invited inside Massachusetts's prisons and mental hospitals to solve.

And one day it hit him. "Universal among the violent criminals was the fact that they were keeping a secret," Gilligan wrote. "A central secret. And that secret was that they felt ashamed—deeply ashamed, chronically ashamed, acutely ashamed." It was shame, every time. "I have yet to see a serious act of violence that was not provoked by the experience of feeling shamed or humiliated, disrespected and ridiculed. As children, these men were shot, axed, scalded, beaten, strangled, tortured, drugged, starved, suffocated, set on fire, thrown out of the window, raped, or prostituted by mothers who were their pimps. For others, words alone shamed and rejected, insulted and humiliated, dishonored and disgraced, tore down their self-esteem, and murdered their soul." For each of them the shaming "occurred on a scale so extreme, so bizarre, and so frequent that one cannot fail to see that the men who occupy the extreme end of the continuum of violent behavior in adulthood occupied an equally extreme end of the continuum of violent child abuse earlier in life."

So they grew up and—"all violence being a person's attempt to replace shame with self-esteem"—they murdered people. One inmate told him, "You wouldn't believe how much respect you get when you have a gun pointed at some dude's face." Gilligan said, "For men who have lived for a lifetime on a diet of contempt and disdain, the temptation to gain instant respect in this way can be worth far more than the cost of going to prison or even of dying."

And after they were jailed, things only got worse. At Walpole—Massachusetts's most riot-prone prison during the 1970s—officers intentionally flooded the cells and put insects in the prisoners' food. They forced inmates to lie face-down before they were allowed meals. Sometimes officers would tell prisoners they had a visitor. Prisoners almost never had visitors, so this was exciting to hear. Then the officer would say that the prisoner didn't really have a visitor and that he was just kidding. And so on.

"They thought these things would be how to get them to

obey," Gilligan told me. "But it did the exact opposite. It stimulated violence."

"Literally, every killer told you this?" I asked. "That the feeling of shame was what led them to do it?"

"It amazed me how universal it was," Gilligan replied. "Over decades."

"What about that pimp from Boston?" I said. "What was his story?"

"His mother had thought he was possessed by the devil," Gilligan said, "so she did voodoo ceremonies and exorcisms in this totally black basement and he was scared to death. He'd shit his pants. He certainly was not loved in any normal sense. His mother had given him this negative identity—that Satan was inside him—so he behaved accordingly." Gilligan paused. "It took some of them a while to confess it to me. It's shameful to have to admit you feel ashamed. By the way, we're saying the word *feeling*. The *feeling* of shame. I think *feeling* is the wrong word."

It may be somewhat paradoxical to refer to shame as a "feeling," for while shame is initially painful, constant shaming leads to a deadening of feeling. Shame, like cold, is, in essence, the absence of warmth. And when it reaches overwhelming intensity, shame is experienced, like cold, as a feeling of numbness and deadness. [In Dante's *Inferno*] the lowest circle of hell was a region not of flames, but of ice—absolute coldness.

—JAMES GILLIGAN, *Violence: Reflections on Our Deadliest Epidemic*

"And finally it struck me," Gilligan said to me. "Our language tells us this. One of the words we use for overwhelming shame is *mortification.* 'I'm mortified.'"

. . .

Their bodies are empty or filled with straw, not flesh and blood . . . Instead of having veins and nerves they have *ropes or cords.*

As Gilligan had said this to me, I remembered a moment from Jonah Lehrer's annihilation. It was when he was standing in front of that giant-screen Twitter feed trying to apologize. Jonah is the sort of person who finds displays of emotion extremely embarrassing, and he then looked deeply uncomfortable.

"I hope that when I tell my young daughter the same story I've just told you," he was saying, "I will be a better person . . ."

"*He is tainted as a writer forever,*" replied the tweets. "*He has not proven that he is capable of feeling shame.*" "*Jonah Lehrer is a friggin' sociopath.*"

Later, when Jonah and I talked about that moment, he told me he had to "turn off some emotional switch in me. I think I had to shut down."

Jonah had a house in the Hollywood Hills and a wife who loved him. He had enough self-esteem to get him through. But I think that in front of the giant Twitter screen he felt for an instant that same deadness that Gilligan's prisoners had described. I have felt it too. I know exactly what Jonah and

Gilligan meant when they talked about shutting down—that moment pain turns to numbness.

. . .

James Gilligan has led a distinguished life. President Clinton and UN Secretary-General Kofi Annan appointed him to sit on advisory committees on the causes of violence. Martin Scorsese based Ben Kingsley's character in *Shutter Island* on him. But for all his accolades, I left Gilligan's apartment thinking that he hadn't considered his life's work a success. There was a time when he might have totally changed the way the United States treated its transgressors. But it didn't happen.

This is the reason why: Throughout the 1980s, Gilligan ran experimental therapeutic communities inside Massachusetts's prisons. They weren't especially radical. They were just about "treating the prisoners with respect," Gilligan told me, "giving people a chance to express their grievances and hopes and wishes and fears." The point was to create an ambience that eradicated shame entirely. "We had one psychiatrist who referred to the inmates as scum. I told him I never wanted to see his face again. It was not only antitherapeutic for the patients, it was dangerous for us." At first, the prison officers had been suspicious, "but eventually some of them began to envy the prisoners," Gilligan said. "Many of them also needed some psychiatric help. These were poorly paid guys, poorly educated. We arranged to get some of them into psychiatric treatment. So they became less insulting and domineering. And violence dropped astoundingly."

Even apparently hopeless cases were transformed, Gilligan said. Even that pimp from Boston. "After he joined our program, he discovered a profoundly retarded eighteen-year-old young man. The boy could hardly tie his shoelaces. So he took care of him. He started protecting him. He'd take him to and from the dining hall. He made sure other inmates didn't harm him. I was, 'Thank God. This could be this guy's road back to humanity.' I told the staff, 'Leave this alone.' Their relationship built and matured. And he has a life now. He has not harmed a hair on anybody's head in twenty-five years. He acts like a normal human being. He's not going anywhere. He's not normal enough to ever go back to the community. But he wouldn't want to. He knows he couldn't make it. He doesn't have the psychological wherewithal, the self-control. But he has reclaimed a level of humanity that I never thought was possible. He works in the prison mental hospital. He's useful to other people. And when I go back to visit, he smiles and says, 'Hello, Dr. Gilligan. How are you?'" Gilligan paused. "I could tell you a hundred stories like that. We'd had men who had blinded themselves by banging their heads against the wall."

In 1991, Gilligan began co-opting Harvard lecturers to donate their time to teach classes inside his prisons. What could be more deshaming than an educational program? His plan coincided with the election of a new governor, William Weld. Weld was asked about Gilligan's initiative in one of his first press conferences. "He said, 'We have to stop this idea of giving free college education to inmates,'" Gilligan told me, "'otherwise people who are too poor to go to college are going to start committing crimes so they can get sent to prison for a free education.'"

And so that was the end of the education program. "He literally decimated it," Gilligan said. "He stripped it. I didn't want to preside over a sham." And so Gilligan quit.

As the years passed, he became for prison reformers a figure of nostalgia. Only a handful of therapeutic communities inspired by his Massachusetts ones exist in American prisons today. But, as it happens, one of them is situated on the top floor of the Hudson County Correctional Center in Kearny, New Jersey. And it is being quietly run by the former New Jersey governor Jim McGreevey.

• • •

The nontherapeutic lower floors of the Hudson County Correctional Center are drab and brown—like the ugly parts of a municipal leisure complex, a long corridor from a changing room to a swimming pool that will never be there. Down here is where New Jersey keeps its suspected immigration offenders. In November 2012 it was declared one of the ten worst immigration detention facilities in America, according to a Detention Watch Network report. Some of the guards down here reportedly called the detainees "animals," and laughed at them, and subjected them to unnecessary strip searches. The report added: "Many immigrants also noted that corrections officers appeared to bring their personal problems to work, taking their frustration and anger out on them."

"EVERY DAY IS A BLESSED DAY!" Jim hollered at a suspected immigration offender who was mopping the floor. The man looked startled. He smiled uneasily.

We kept walking—past inmates just sitting there, looking at walls. "Normal prison is punishment in the worst sense," Jim told me. "It's like a soul-bleeding. Day in, day out, people find themselves doing virtually nothing in a very negative environment."

I thought of Lindsey Stone, just sitting at her kitchen table for almost a year, staring at the online shamings of people just like her.

"People move away from themselves," Jim said. "Inmates tell me time and again that they feel themselves shutting down, building a wall."

Jim and I walked into an elevator. An inmate was already in there. Everyone was quiet.

"Every day is a blessed day," said Jim.

More silence.

"Watch your character! It becomes your destiny!" said Jim.

We reached the top floor. The doors opened.

"You go first," said Jim.

"Oh, no, please, you," said the inmate.

"No, you," said Jim.

"Oh, no, you," said the inmate.

We all stood there. The inmate went first. Jim gave me a happy smile.

The first time I'd met Jim—when he'd yelled "STUDY

HARD AT MATH!" at a startled stranger child—I'd found him a bit nuts. But somewhere along the line he'd become heroic to me. I'd been thinking about a message that had appeared on the giant Twitter feed behind Jonah's head: *"He is tainted as a writer forever."* And a tweet directed at Justine Sacco: *"Your tweet lives on forever."* The word *forever* had been coming up a lot during my two years among the publicly shamed. Jonah and Justine and people like them were being told, "No. There is no door. There is no way back in. We don't offer any forgiveness." But we know that people are complicated and have a mixture of flaws and talents and sins. So why do we pretend that we don't?

Amid all the agony, Jim McGreevey was trying an extraordinary thing.

In front of us was a giant locked dormitory room. Inside were forty women. This was Jim's therapeutic unit. We waited for someone to let us in. It wasn't like downstairs, Jim said; his women were "up at eight-thirty a.m. They all have chores. Everybody works. They're all assigned physical tasks. Then there are workshops—on sex abuse, domestic violence, anger management—then lunch, then in the afternoon they focus in on job training, housing. There are books. There's cake. There's the library. Then the mothers can read bedtime nursery rhymes to their children over Skype."

There were glimpses of a summer day through the windows, and as a corrections officer let us in, she said that tensions were high because warm days are when a person really feels incarcerated.

———

Jim gathered the women into a circle for a group meeting. I wasn't allowed to record it and so I managed only to scribble down fragments of conversations like "I come from a small town so everyone knows where I am and that tears me up inside . . ." and "most people know why *Raquel* is in here . . ."

At that, a few women glanced over at the woman I took to be Raquel. Their looks seemed wary and deferential. Pretty much every woman here was in for drugs or prostitution. But the comment and the glances made me think that with Raquel it was something else.

Raquel's eyes darted around the room. She fidgeted a lot. The other women were stiller. I wondered what Raquel had done, but I didn't know the etiquette of how to ask. Then, as soon as the meeting broke up, Raquel immediately dashed across the room to me and told me everything. I somehow managed to get it all down—taking notes frantically like a secretary in *Mad Men*.

"I was born in Puerto Rico," she said. "I was sexually abused from the age of four. When I was six, we moved to New Jersey. Every memory I have of growing up is a memory of being punched in the face and told I was worthless. When I was fifteen, my brother broke my nose. I ended up covered in blood. When I was sixteen, I had my first boyfriend. Three months later I was married. I started smoking pot, drinking. I cheated on my husband. I left him. Eighteen, nineteen was a big blur. I tried heroin. Thank God I don't have an addictive personality. I drank like a fish. We'd go to bars, wait for people to come out, take their money, and make fun of how they screamed for their moms. Suddenly, holy shit, I'm pregnant. I'm pregnant with the only thing that's ever going to love me. My son was born January 25, 1996. I went to business school, dropped out. I had a daughter. We moved to Florida. In Florida we'd have water fights, movie nights. I'd buy all their favorite food and lay it all out on the bed and we'd pile in and watch movies until we all passed out. We played baseball in the rain. My son loves comedy, drama, he sings. He won a talent show when he was fourteen. I would make him do his homework over and over. I used to make him do five-page reports, read encyclopedias. I shoved him out of the bed when he was fourteen and slapped him. A girl had texted him, 'Are you a virgin?' I was ballistic. I slapped the shit out of him. It left nail marks."

Ten months ago Raquel had sent her children to stay with their father in Florida for a vacation. As she watched them walk down the tunnel toward the plane, her son suddenly turned and called back at her, "How much do you want to bet I don't come back?" Then he said, "Just kidding."

Raquel yelled back at him, "How much do you want to bet you don't get on that plane?"

Her son walked on for a few more steps. Then he called back, "We should make that bet."

"And that was the last thing he ever said to me," Raquel said.

That Friday the Department of Children and Families turned
up at Raquel's house. Her son was accusing her of child abuse.
"He used to ask me if he could stay out until nine p.m,"
Raquel said. "I'd say no. He'd ask why not. I'd say, 'There are
people out there that can hurt you.' But I was hurting him
more than anyone. Thank God they got away from me when
they did. He's safe. He's getting the chance to be a teenager.
He's a very angry boy because I made him that way. My
daughter is very shy, withdrawn, because I made her that way.
I just pray they'll be normal."

For the first few months of Raquel's incarceration she was
downstairs on a nontherapeutic floor.

"What was that like?" I asked her.

"Downstairs is chaos," she replied. "It's borderline bar-
baric. Downstairs girls get slapped with the food trays. Some
girl will decide she doesn't like you. She'll pull you into a
room and lock the door and you'll fight and whoever comes
out unbroken wins. Up here we eat coffee cake. We watch TV.
We spread books across the table. It's like we're in a college
cafeteria sipping our coffee. Sophisticated!"

Just then there was commotion. A woman behind us had
collapsed and was having a seizure. She was carried away on
a stretcher.

"Feel better!" some of the other women shouted after her.

"Last call for medications," an officer called out.

Jim and I left the prison and walked back toward his car.

"How long do you think Raquel will stay in prison?" I asked him.

"We'll know more in two weeks," he replied. "That's when we're due to hear from the prosecutor. My guess is a few more months."

Jim said he'd pass on the news when he heard it. Then he drove me to the train station.

I didn't hear from Jim two weeks later, so I e-mailed: "How did things go with Raquel?"

Jim e-mailed back. "She received difficult news yesterday. An eight-count indictment. She is in significant emotional pain."

I telephoned him. "What are they charging her with?" I asked.

"Attempted murder in the first degree," Jim replied. He sounded shaken. "She threw a knife at her son. They're going for a twenty-year jail sentence."

● ● ●

Six months later. Three people sat together in the council chamber at Newark City Hall: Jim, Raquel, and I.

Jim had intervened. The prosecutors were persuaded that Raquel was a victim of an "abuse cycle." And so instead of twenty years she served four more months and then they let her go.

"If shaming worked, if prison worked, then it would work," Jim said to me. "But it doesn't work." He paused. "Look, some people need to go to prison forever. Some people are incapable . . . but most people . . ."

"It's disorienting," I said, "that the line between hell and redemption in the U.S. justice system is so fine."

"It's public defenders that are overwhelmed and prosecutors that are following guidelines," Jim said.

This has been a book about people who really didn't do very much wrong. Justine and Lindsey, certainly, were destroyed for nothing more than telling bad jokes. And while we were busy steadfastly refusing them forgiveness, Jim was quietly arranging the salvation of someone who had committed a far more serious offense. It struck me that if deshaming would work for a maelstrom like Raquel, if it would restore someone like her to health, then we need to think twice about raining down vengeance and anger as our default position.

It wasn't freedom without boundaries for Raquel. She'd been banned from contacting her children for five years. Her son would be twenty-two then, her daughter seventeen. "So even when she's seventeen, any contact will have to be okayed with their father," Raquel told me, "because my parental rights have been stripped." But still, she gets updates. "My friends from Florida are still friends with them. My friend actually called me yesterday and said, 'You will never guess who is Facebooking me right now.' I said, 'Who?' She said, 'Your daughter.' I said, 'No way!' My daughter is sending her messages, and she's sitting there reading them to me. So apparently my daughter has a little crush on someone. He's got a cleft in his chin. He's got sandy brown hair . . .'"

I told Raquel it was nice to see her in such a good mood. And that's when she told me her news.

"Yesterday, when group was over, Miss Blake called me into her office."

Miss Blake was the manager of Raquel's halfway house.

"She said, 'Raquel, I've seen how you carry yourself, how the guys listen to you. I want to offer you a job here. Can you get me your résumé?'"

Raquel replied, "As luck would have it, I have a résumé right here."

Then Raquel said, "Miss Blake, is this really happening?"

And Miss Blake nodded.

. . .

got a call from Michael Fertik's people. They were ready to start on Lindsey Stone.

Fourteen

Cats and Ice Cream and Music

A re there any hobbies you're particularly passionate about right now? Marathons? Photography?"

Farukh Rashid in San Francisco was talking on a conference line to Lindsey Stone. I was listening in from my sofa in New York.

I'd met Farukh a few months earlier when Michael's publicist, Leslie Hobbs, gave me a tour of the Reputation.com offices—two open-plan floors with soundproofed booths for sensitive calls to celebrity clients. She introduced me to Farukh and explained that he usually works on Michael's VIP customers—the CEOs and celebrities.

"It's nice that you're giving Lindsey the bespoke service," I said.

"She needs it," Leslie replied.

She really did. Michael's strategists had been researching Lindsey's online life and had discovered literally nothing about her besides that "silence and respect" incident.

"That five seconds of her life is her entire Internet presence?" I said.

Farukh nodded. "And it's not just this Lindsey Stone. Anyone who has that name has the same problem. There are sixty Lindsey Stones in the U.S. There's a designer in Austin, Texas, a photographer, there's even a gymnast, and they're all being defined by that one photograph."

"I'm sorry to have given you such a tricky one," I said, feeling a little proud of myself.

"Oh, no, we're excited," Farukh replied. "It's a challenging scenario but a great scenario. We're going to introduce the Internet to the real Lindsey Stone."

"Are cats important to you?" Farukh asked Lindsey on the conference call.

"Absolutely," said Lindsey.

I heard Farukh type the word *cats* into his computer. Farukh was young and energetic and just as upbeat and buoyant and lacking in cynicism and malevolent irony as he was hoping to make Lindsey seem. His Twitter profile said he enjoys "biking, hiking, and family time." His plan was to create Lindsey Stone Tumblrs and LinkedIn pages and WordPress blogs and Instagram accounts and YouTube accounts to overwhelm that terrible photograph, wash it away in a tidal wave of positivity, away to a place on Google where normal people don't look—a place like page two of the search results. According to Google's own research into our "eye movements," 53 percent of us don't go beyond the first two search results, and 89 percent don't look down past the first page.

"What the first page looks like," Michael's strategist, Jered Higgins, told me during my tour of their offices, "determines what people think of you."

As a writer and journalist—as well as a father and human being—this struck me as a really horrifying way of knowing the world.

"I'm passionate about music," Lindsey told Farukh. "I like Top 40 chart music."

"That's really good," said Farukh. "Let's work with that. Do you play an instrument?"

"I used to," Lindsey said. "I was kind of self-taught. It's just something I mess around with. It's not anything I . . ." At first, she'd sounded like she'd been enjoying the fun of it all, but now she seemed self-conscious, like the endeavor was giving her troubling existential thoughts—questions like "Who *am* I?" and "What are we *doing*?"

"I'm having a hard time with this," she said. "As a normal person I don't really know how to . . . brand myself online. I'm trying to come up with things for you guys to write about. But it's hard, you know?"

"Piano? Guitar? Drums?" said Farukh. "Or travel? Where do you go?"

"I don't know," Lindsey said. "I go to the cave. I go to the beach. I get ice cream."

At Farukh's request, Lindsey had been e-mailing him photographs that didn't involve her inadvertently flipping off military cemeteries. She'd been providing biographical details too. Her favorite TV show was *Parks and Recreation*. Her employment history included five years at Walmart, "which was kind of soul-suckingly awful."

"Are you sure you want to say that Walmart was soul-sucking?" Farukh said.

"Oh . . . What? Really?" Lindsey laughed as if to say, "Come on! Everyone knows that about Walmart!" But then she hesitated.

The conference call was proving an unexpectedly melancholic experience. It was nothing to do with Farukh. He really felt for Lindsey and wanted to do a good job for her. The sad thing was that Lindsey had incurred the Internet's wrath because she was impudent and playful and foolhardy and outspoken. And now here she was, working with Farukh to reduce herself to safe banalities—to cats and ice cream and Top 40 chart music. We were creating a world where the smartest way to survive is to be bland.

• • •

There was a time when Michael Fertik wouldn't have needed to be so calculating. Back in the mid-1990s search engines were interested only in how many times a particular keyword appeared within a page. To be the number-one Jon Ronson search term on AltaVista or HotBot, you just had to write "Jon Ronson" over and over again. Which for me would be the most fantastic website to chance upon, but for everyone else, less so.

But then two students at Stanford, Larry Page and Sergey

Brin, had their idea. Why not build a search engine that ranked websites by popularity instead? If someone is linking to your page, that's one vote. A link, they figured, is like a citation—a nod of respect. If the page linking to your page has a lot of links into it, then that page counts for more votes. An esteemed person bestowing their admiration on you is worth more than some loner doing the same. And that was it. They called their invention PageRank, after Larry Page, and as soon as they turned the algorithm on, we early searchers were spellbound.

This was why Farukh needed to create LinkedIn and Tumblr and Twitter pages for Lindsey. They come with a built-in high PageRank. The Google algorithm prejudges them as well liked. But for Michael Fertik, the problem with Google is that it is forever evolving—adjusting its algorithm in ways it keeps secret.

"Google is a tricky beast and a moving target," Michael told me. "And so we try to decipher it, to reverse engineer it."

This was what Michael knew right now: "Google tends to like stuff that's old. It seems to think old stuff has a certain authority. And Google tends to like stuff that's new. With the intervening stuff, week six, week twelve, there's a dip." Which was why Michael's people predicted that Lindsey's love of cats or whatever would achieve "initial strong impact," followed by "fluctuation." And after fluctuation: "reversion."

Michael's clients dread reversion. There's nothing more dispiriting than seeing the nice new judgments disappear down to page two and the horrific old judgments bubble back up again. But reversion is actually their friend, Jered Higgins told me. Reversion is when you think Glenn Close is dead but she suddenly leaps up in the bath, apparently filled with a new violent fervor, but really she's muddled and wounded and vulnerable.

"Reversion shows that the algorithm is uncertain," Jered said. "It's the algorithm shifting things around and wondering what, from a mathematical standpoint, is the story that needs to be told about this person."

And during this uncertainty, Jered said, "we go in and blast it."

The blasting—the bombardment of the algorithm with Tumblr pages about Lindsey's trips to the beach, the shock and awe of these pleasant banalities—has to be choreographed just right. Google knows if it's being manipulated. Alarm bells go off. "So we have a strategic schedule for content creation and publication," Jered said. "We create a natural-looking activity online. That's a lot of accumulated intelligence."

. . .

M ichael Fertik took me for dinner and he talked to me about the criticism that people often level at him, that "any change of search results is manipulating truth and chilling free speech." He drank some wine. "But there is a chilling of behavior that goes along with a virtual lynching. There is a life modification."

"I know," I said. "For a year Lindsey Stone had felt too plagued to even go to karaoke." And karaoke is something you do alone in a room with your friends.

"And that's not an unusual reaction," Michael said. "People change their phone numbers. They don't leave the house. They go into therapy. They have signs of PTSD. It's like the Stasi. We're creating a culture where people feel constantly surveilled, where people are afraid to be themselves."

"Like the NSA," I said.

"This is more frightening than the NSA," said Michael. "The NSA is looking for terrorists. They're not getting psychosexual pleasure out of their schadenfreude about you."

I wondered what to make of Michael's Stasi analogy. There's an old Internet adage that as soon as you compare something to the Nazis you lose the argument. Maybe the same could be said about the Stasi—the East Germans' secret police force during the Cold War. They would, after all, creep into the homes of suspected enemies of the state and spray radiation onto them as they slept, their idea being to use the radiation as a tracking device. Stasi agents would follow them through crowds, pointing Geiger counters at them. A lot of suspected enemies of the state died of unusual cancers during the Stasi's reign.

But the Stasi didn't only inflict physical horror. Their main endeavor was to create the most elaborate surveillance network in world history. It didn't seem unreasonable to scrutinize this aspect of them in the hope it might teach us something about our own social media surveillance network.

In Anna Funder's seminal history of the Stasi—*Stasiland*—she interviews a woman named Julia who was one day called in for interrogation. The Stasi had intercepted love letters between her and her Western boyfriend. They were sitting on the officer's desk in the interrogation room.

> There was a pile of her letters to the Italian. There was a pile of his letters back to her. This man knew everything. He could see when she had doubts. He could see by what sweet-talking she had let herself be placated. He could see the Italian boyfriend's longing laid bare.

Julia told Anna Funder that she was "definitely psychologically damaged" by the incident—the way the officer read through her letters in front of her, making little comments. "That's probably why I react so extremely to approaches from men. I experience them as another possible invasion of my intimate sphere."

Anna Funder wrote *Stasiland* back in 2003—fourteen years after the fall of the Stasi and three years before the invention of Twitter. Of course, no prurient or censorious bureaucrat had intercepted Justine Sacco's private thoughts. Justine had tweeted them herself, laboring under the misapprehension—the same one I labored under for a while—that Twitter was a safe place to tell the truth about yourself to strangers. That truth telling had really proven to be an idealistic experiment gone wrong.

Anna Funder visited a Stasi officer whose job had been to co-opt informants. She wanted to know how—given that informant pay was terrible, and the workload was ever burgeoning, with more and more behaviors getting redefined as enemy activities—he managed to persuade people to get on board.

"Mostly people just said yes," he told her.

"Why?" she asked him.

"Some of them were convinced of the cause," he said. "But I think mainly because informers felt they *were* somebody, you know? Someone was listening to them for a couple of hours every week, taking notes. They felt they had it over other people."

That struck me as a condescending thing for the Stasi man to say about his informants. And it would be a condescending thing to say about Twitter users too. Social media gives a voice to voiceless people—its egalitarianism is its greatest quality. But I was struck by a report Anna Funder discovered that had been written by a Stasi psychologist tasked with trying to understand why they were attracting so many willing informants. His conclusion: "It was an impulse to make sure your neighbor was doing the right thing."

In October 2014, I took a final drive up to visit Lindsey Stone. Four months had passed since I'd last spoken to her or Farukh—I hadn't called them and they hadn't called me—and given that they'd taken her on only for my benefit, I'd half wondered if maybe it had all been quietly wound down in my absence.

"Oh God, no," said Lindsey. We sat at her kitchen table. "They call me every week, week after week. You didn't know that?"

"No," I said.

"I thought you guys were talking all the time," she said.

Lindsey got out her phone and scrolled through her innumerable e-mails from Farukh. She read out loud some blog posts his team had written in her voice, about how it's important when traveling to use the hotel safe—"Stay alert, travelers!"—and how if you're in Spain you should try the tapas.

Lindsey got to preapprove everything and she'd told them no only twice, she said: to the post about how much she was looking forward to Lady Gaga's upcoming jazz album ("I like Lady Gaga, but I'm not really excited about her jazz album") and to her tribute to Disneyland on the occasion of its fiftieth birthday: "Happy Birthday, Disneyland! The Happiest Place on Earth!"

"'Happy Birthday, Disneyland!'" Lindsey blushed. "I would never . . . I mean, I had a great time at Disneyland . . ."

"Who doesn't?" I said.

"But still . . ." Lindsey trailed off.

After we both laughed about the "Happy Birthday, Disneyland" blog post, we both stopped laughing and felt bad.

"They're working so hard," Lindsey said.

"And it's what they have to do," I said.

"Yeah," Lindsey said. "One of my friends from high school said, 'I hope it's still *you*. I want people to know how funny you are.' But it's scary. After all that's happened, what's funny to me . . . I don't want to go anywhere near the line, let alone cross it. So I'm constantly saying, 'I don't know, Farukh, what do you think?'"

"This journey started with my identity being hijacked by

a spambot," I said. "Your personality has been taken by strangers twice now. But at least this second time around it's nice."

Lindsey hadn't typed her name into Google for eleven months. The last time had been a shock. It was Veterans Day and she discovered some ex–army people "wondering where I was, and not in a good way."

"They were thinking about tracking you down so they could re-destroy you?" I asked.

"Yeah," she said.

She hadn't looked since. And now she swallowed and began to type: L . . . I . . . N . . .

Lindsey shook her head, stunned. "This is monumental," she said.

Two years before, the photograph stretched to Google Images' horizon—uninterrupted mass-production shaming, "pages and pages and pages," Lindsey said, "repeating end-lessly. It felt so huge. So oppressive."

And now: gone.

Well—nearly gone. There was still a scattering of them, maybe three or four, but they were interspersed with lots of photographs of Lindsey doing nothing bad. Just smiling. Even better, there were lots of photographs of *other* Lindsey Stones—people who weren't her at all. There was a Lind-sey Stone volleyball player, a Lindsay Stone competitive swimmer (the different spelling didn't seem to matter to Google Images). The swimmer had been captured mid-stroke, moments from winning the New York State 500-yard freestyle championship. The photo was captioned: "Lindsay Stone had the right plan in place and everything was going exactly to plan."

A whole other person, doing something everyone could agree was lovely and commendable. There was no better result than that.

Fifteen

Your Speed

We have always had some influence over the justice system, but for the first time in 180 years—since the stocks and the pillory were outlawed—we have the power to determine the severity of some punishments. And so we have to think about what level of mercilessness we feel comfortable with. I, personally, no longer take part in the ecstatic public condemnation of people unless they've committed a transgression that has an actual victim, and even then not as much as I probably should. I miss the fun a little. But it feels like when I became a vegetarian. I missed the steak, although not as much as I'd anticipated, but I could no longer ignore the slaughterhouse.

———

I kept remembering something Michael Fertik had said to me at the Village Pub in Woodside. "The biggest lie," he said, "is, *The Internet is about you.*" We like to think of ourselves as people who have choice and taste and personalized content. But the Internet isn't about us. It's about the companies that dominate the data flows of the Internet."

Now I suddenly wondered. Did Google make money from the destruction of Justine Sacco? Could a figure be calculated? And so I joined forces with a number-crunching researcher, Solvej Krause, and began writing to economists and analysts and online-ad-revenue people.

Some things were known. In December 2013, the month of Justine's annihilation, 12.2 billion Google searches took place—a figure that made me feel less worried about the possibility that people were sitting inside Google headquarters personally judging me. Google's ad revenue for that month was $4.69 billion. Which meant they made an average of thirty-eight cents for every search query. Every time we typed anything into Google: thirty-eight cents to Google. Of those 12.2 billion searches that December, 1.2 million were people searching the name Justine Sacco. And so, if you average it out, Justine's catastrophe instantaneously made Google $456,000.

But it wouldn't be accurate to simply multiply 1.2 million by thirty-eight cents. Some searches are worth far more to Google than others. Advertisers bid on "high-yield" search terms like "Coldplay" and "jewelry" and "Kenya vacations." It's quite possible that no advertiser ever linked its product to Justine's name. But that wouldn't mean Google made no money from her. Justine was the worldwide number-one trending topic on Twitter. Her story engrossed social media users more than any other that night. I think people who wouldn't otherwise have gone onto Google did specifically to hunt for her. She drew people in. And once they were there, I'm sure at least a few of them decided to book a Kenya vacation or download a Coldplay album.

I got an e-mail from the economics researcher Jonathan Hersh. He'd come recommended by the people who make *Freakonomics Radio* on WNYC. Jonathan's e-mail said the same thing: "Something about this story resonated with them, so much so that they felt compelled to google her name. That means they're engaged. If interest in Justine were sufficient to encourage users to stay online for more time than they would otherwise, this would have directly resulted in Google making more advertising revenue. Google has the informal corporate motto of 'Don't be evil,' but they make money when *anything* happens online, even the bad stuff."

In the absence of any better data from Google, he wrote, he could only offer a "back of the envelope" calculation. But he thought it would be appropriately conservative—maybe a little *too* conservative—to estimate Justine's worth, being a "low-value query," at a quarter of the average. Which, if true, means Google made $120,000 from the destruction of Justine Sacco.

Maybe that's an accurate figure. Or maybe Google made more. But one thing's certain. Those of us who did the actual annihilating? We got nothing.

• • •

From the beginning, I'd been trying to understand why—once you discount Gustave LeBon and Philip Zimbardo's theories of viruses and contagion and evil—online shaming is so pitiless. And now I think I have the answer. I found it in, of all places, an article about a radical traffic-calming scheme tested in California in the early 2000s. The story—by the journalist Thomas Goetz—is a fantastically esoteric one. Goetz writes about how in the school zones of Garden Grove, California, cars were ignoring speed signs and hitting "bicyclists and pedestrians with depressing regularity." And so they tried something experimental. They tried Your Speed signs.

After I read Thomas Goetz's article about Your Speed signs, I spent a long time trying to track down their inventor. He

turned out to be an Oregon road-sign manufacturer named Scott Kelley.

"I remember exactly where I was when I thought of them," he told me over the telephone. "It was the mid-1990s. I was over by my girlfriend's house. I was driving through a school zone. And my mind just pictured one of the signs up on a pole."

"What made you think they'd work?" I asked him. "There was nothing about them to suggest they'd work."

"Right," said Scott. "And that's where it gets interesting."

They really, logically, shouldn't have worked. As Thomas Goetz writes:

> The signs were curious in a few ways. For one thing, they didn't tell drivers anything they didn't already know—there is, after all, a speedometer in every car. If a motorist wanted to know their speed, a glance at the dashboard would do it . . . And the Your Speed signs came with no punitive follow-up—no police officer standing by ready to write a ticket. This defied decades of law-enforcement dogma, which held that most people obey speed limits only if they face some clear negative consequence for exceeding them.
>
> In other words, officials in Garden Grove were betting that giving speeders redundant information with no consequence would somehow compel them to do something few of us are inclined to do: slow down.

Scott Kelley's idea, being so counterintuitive, proved a marketing nightmare. No town official anywhere in America was placing orders. So he did the only thing he could—he sent out free samples for testing. One ended up in his own neighborhood.

"I remember driving by it," he said. "And I slowed down. I knew there was no camera in it taking my picture. Yet I slowed down. I just went, 'Wow! This really does work!'"

In test after test the results came back the same. People did slow down—by an average of 14 percent. And they stayed slowed down for miles down the road.

"So *why* do they work?" I asked Scott.

His reply surprised me. "I don't know," he said. "I really don't know. I . . . Yeah. I don't know."

Scott explained that, being a tech person, he was more interested in the radar and the casing and the lightbulbs than in the psychology. But during the past decade, the mystery has galvanized social psychologists. And their conclusion: feedback loops.

Feedback loops. You exhibit some type of behavior (you drive at twenty-seven miles per hour in a twenty-five-mile-an-hour zone). You get instant real-time feedback for it (the sign tells you you're driving at twenty-seven miles per hour). You decide whether or not to change your behavior as a result of the feedback (you lower your speed to twenty-five miles per hour). You get instant feedback for that decision too (the sign tells you you're driving at twenty-five miles per hour now, and some signs flash up a smiley-face emoticon to congratulate you). And it all happens in the flash of an eye—in the few moments it takes you to drive past the Your Speed sign.

In Goetz's *Wired* magazine story—"Harnessing the Power of Feedback Loops"—he calls them "a profoundly effective tool for changing behavior." And I'm all for people slowing down in school zones. But maybe in other ways feedback loops are leading to a world we only think we want. Maybe— as my friend the documentary maker Adam Curtis e-mailed me—they're turning social media into "a giant echo chamber where what we believe is constantly reinforced by people who believe the same thing."

We express our opinion that Justine Sacco is a monster. We are instantly congratulated for this—for basically being Rosa Parks. We make the on-the-spot decision to carry on believing it.

"The tech-utopians like the people in *Wired* present this as a new kind of democracy," Adam's e-mail continued. "It isn't. It's the opposite. It locks people off in the world they started with and prevents them from finding out anything different. They got trapped in the system of feedback reinforcement. The idea that there is another world of other people who have other ideas is marginalized in our lives."

I was becoming one of those other people with other ideas. I was expressing the unpopular belief that Justine Sacco isn't a monster. I wonder if I will receive a tidal wave of negative feedback for this and, if so, will it frighten me back again, to a place where I'm congratulated and welcomed?

"Feedback is an engineering principle," Adam's e-mail to me ended. "And all engineering is devoted to trying to keep the thing you are building stable."

Soon after Justine Sacco's shaming, I was talking with a friend, a journalist, who told me he had so many jokes, little observations, potentially risqué thoughts, that he wouldn't dare to post online anymore.

"I suddenly feel with social media like I'm tiptoeing around an unpredictable, angry, unbalanced parent who might strike out at any moment," he said. "It's horrible."

He didn't want me to name him, he said, in case it sparked something off.

We see ourselves as nonconformist, but I think all of this is creating a more conformist, conservative age.

"Look!" we're saying. "WE'RE normal! THIS is the average!"

We are defining the boundaries of normality by tearing apart the people outside it.

Bibliography and Acknowledgments

A note about the title. For a while it was going to be, simply, *Shame*. Or *Tarred and Feathered*. There was a lot of to-ing and fro-ing. It was a surprisingly hard book to find a title for, and I think I know why. It was something that one of my interviewees said to me: "Shame is an incredibly inarticulate emotion. It's something you bathe in, it's not something you wax eloquent about. It's such a deep, dark, ugly thing there are very few words for it."

My encounter with the spambot men was filmed by Remy Lamont of Channel Flip. My thanks to him, and to Channel Flip, and, as always, to my producer Lucy Greenwell. Greg Stekelman—formally known as @themanwhofell—helped me remember how Twitter mutated from a place of unselfconscious honesty into something more anxiety-inducing. Greg is not on Twitter anymore. His final tweet, posted on May 10, 2012, reads: "Twitter is no place for a human being."

Which I think is pessimistic. I still love the place. Although I've never been shamed on it. Although neither has he. That line about how we don't feel accountable during a shaming because "a snowflake never feels responsible for the avalanche" came from Jonathan Bullock. My thanks to him.

I pieced together the story of how Michael Moynihan uncovered Jonah Lehrer's deception mainly through my interviews with Michael—my thanks to him and to his wife, Joanne—though a little background came from "Michael C. Moynihan, The Guy Who Uncovered Jonah Lehrer's Fabrication Problem," by Foster Kamer, published in *The New York Observer* on July 30, 2012.

My information about Stephen Glass came from "No Second Chance for Stephen Glass: The Long, Strange Downfall of a Journalistic Wunderkind," by Adam L. Penenberg, published by *PandoDaily* on January 27, 2014.

The story about Jonah's trip to St. Louis the day before his downfall came from "Jonah Lehrer Stumbles at MPI," by Sarah J. F. Braley, published on Meetings-conventions.com on August 2, 2012. In a telephone interview, Jonah Lehrer spoke with me at length and on the record. After our telephone interview, however, he expressed misgivings about being included in the book, saying he didn't want to put his wife and family through the experience again. But his experience was too vital and too public—and the lesons learned too great—to leave out.

Thanks to Jeff Bercovici of *Forbes* magazine for putting me in touch with his friend Justine Sacco.

The life and work of Judge Ted Poe has been documented

over the years by his nemesis the legal scholar Jonathan Turley in stories such as "Shame on You," published in *The Washington Post* on September 18, 2005. I learned about the drunk drivers Mike Hubacek and Kevin Tunell from reading "A Great Crime Deterrent," by Julia Duin, published in *Insight on the News* on October 19, 1998, and "Kevin Tunell Is Paying $1 a Week for a Death He Caused and Finding the Price Unexpectedly High," by Bill Hewitt and Tom Nugent, published in *People* magazine on April 16, 1990.

I loved piecing together the history of group madness from Gustave LeBon to Philip Zimbardo. Five people were incredibly generous with their time and expertise—Adam Curtis, Bob Nye, Steve Reicher, Alex Haslam, and, especially, Clifford Stott. Clifford kindly talked me through the perils of deindividuation in two long Skype conversations. I recommend his book *Mad Mobs and Englishmen? Myths and Realities of the 2011 Riots*, cowritten with Steve Reicher and published by Constable & Robinson in 2011.

My research into LeBon's history took me to Bob Nye's book *The Origins of Crowd Psychology: Gustave LeBon and the Crisis of Mass Democracy in the 3rd Republic*, issued by SAGE Publications in 1975, and to Nye's introduction to the Transaction Publishers' reprint of the Dover edition of Gustave LeBon's *The Crowd*, published in 1995. Some details about LeBon's relationship with the Anthropological Society of Paris came from *Nature and Nurture in French Social Sciences, 1859–1914 and Beyond*, by Martin S. Staum, published by McGill–Queen's University Press in 2011. I learned that LeBon's fans included Goebbels and Mussolini from reading

Fascist Spectacle: The Aesthetics of Power in Mussolini's Italy, written by Simonetta Falasca-Zamponi and published by the University of California Press in 2000, and *The Third Reich: Politics and Propaganda,* written by David Welch and published by Routledge in 2002.

My research into Philip Zimbardo took me to "Rethinking the Psychology of Tyranny: The BBC Prison Study," by Steve Reicher and Alex Haslam, which appeared in the *British Journal of Social Psychology* in 2006, and Dr. Zimbardo's rebuttal, "On Rethinking the Psychology of Tyranny: The BBC Prison Study," published in the same journal.

Dr. Gary Slutkin's comments about the London riots being like a virus came from his article "Rioting Is a Disease Spread from Person to Person—The Key Is to Stop the Infection," published in *The Observer/The Guardian* on August 13, 2011. The Jack Levin quotation came from "UK Riots: 'We Don't Want No Trouble. We Just Want a Job,'" written by Shiv Malik and published in *The Guardian* on August 12, 2011. It was Clifford Stott's book and guidance that took me to both of those stories.

My interview with Malcolm Gladwell was broadcast on BBC's *The Culture Show* on October 2, 2013. My thanks to the director, Colette Camden; the series producer, Emma Cahusac; and the series editor, Janet Lee.

Although this book is full of new stuff, a few lines were self-plagiarized from a column and a feature I wrote for *The Guardian's Weekend* magazine. I'm referring to the story of how my son forced me to reenact being thrown into a lake, and to my interviews with Troy and Mercedes Haefer from 4chan. Parts of those interviews appeared in my story "Security Alert," which was published in *The Guardian* on May 3, 2013. My thanks to Charlotte Northedge, who edited that feature.

My information about Oswald Mosley and Diana Mitford came from *The Mitfords: Letters Between Six Sisters*, edited by Charlotte Mosley and published by 4th Estate in 2007, and from *Hurrah for the Blackshirts! Fascists and Fascism in Britain Between the Wars*, written by Martin Pugh and published by Jonathan Cape in 2005. I'd also like to thank Jil Cove of the Cable Street Group, a history project created to commemorate those people who fought back against the British Union of Fascists. Some biographical details about Max Mosley came from his interview with John Humphreys on BBC Radio 4's *On the Ropes*, which was broadcast on March 1, 2011, and from "Max Mosley Fights Back," by Lucy Kellaway, published in the *Financial Times* on February 4, 2011. I drew as well from Justice David Eady's July 24, 2008, adjudication on *Max Mosley v. News Group Newspapers Ltd*, which can be read on bbc.co.uk.

I learned about the suicide of the Welsh lay preacher Arnold Lewis from three sources: *News of the World? Fake Sheikhs and Royal Trappings*, written by Peter Burden and published by Eye Books in 2009; *Tickle the Public: One Hundred Years of the Popular Press*, written by Matthew Engel and published by Phoenix in 1997; and Ian Cutler's self-published memoir *The Camera Assassin III: Confessions of a Gutter Press Photojournalist*, which is available for free on his website—www.cameraassassin.co.uk.

I first learned about David Buss—the author of *The Murderer Next Door*—from *Radiolab: The Bad Show*, first broadcast on WNYC on January 9, 2012. It was a producer of *Radiolab*—Tim Howard—who put me in touch with a former contributor to the show, Jonah Lehrer. So my thanks to *Radiolab* for that too. *The Murderer Next Door* was published by the Penguin Press in 2005.

Some background information on the Zumba prostitution ring in Kennebunk came from the story "Modern-Day Puritans Wring Hands over Zumba Madam's List of Shame," by Patrik Jonsson, which appeared in *The Christian Science Monitor* on October 13, 2012.

For more on Larry Page and Sergey Brin's days at Stanford, I recommend "The Birth of Google," by John Battelle, which appeared in *Wired* in August 2005.

All my information about the Stasi came from Anna Funder's brilliant *Stasiland: Stories from Behind the Berlin Wall*, published by Granta in 2003 and reprinted by Harper Perennial in 2011.

My research into the terrible story of Lindsay Armstrong took me to "She Couldn't Take Any More," by Kirsty Scott, published in *The Guardian* on August 1, 2002. My thanks to Kirsty for her article and for her help putting me in touch with Lindsay's mother, Linda.

Biographical information about Jim McGreevey came from his memoir *The Confession*, published by William Morrow Paperbacks in 2007.

For more on Walpole Prison during the 1970s, I recommend *When the Prisoners Ran Walpole: A True Story in the Movement for Prison Abolition*, by Jamie Bissonnette, with Ralph Hamm, Robert Dellelo, and Edward Rodman, published by South End Press in 2008, and James Gilligan's

Violence: Reflections on a National Epidemic, published by Vintage in 1997. In 1981, Massachusetts state senator Jack Backman wrote an open letter to Amnesty International complaining about conditions inside Walpole. I used a few lines from his letter in my description of life inside the prison. My thanks to Backman's former aide S. Brian Wilson for publishing it online.

A huge number of economists and journalists and ad-revenue people offered to help me understand how Google may have profited from the shaming of Justine Sacco. I'm very grateful to them all—Chris Bannon, Aarti Shahani, Jeremy Gin, Ruth Lewy, Solvej Krause, Rebecca Watson, Paul Zak, Darren Filson, Brian Lance, Jonathan Hersh, Alex Blumberg, Steve Henn, and Zoe Chace.

My thanks to Thomas Goetz for his help in tracking down the inventor of Your Speed signs.

My wife, Elaine, was a brilliant early reader, as were my editors, Geoff Kloske at Riverhead, Kris Doyle and Paul Baggaley at Picador, and Natasha Fairweather and Natasha Galloway at AP Watt/United Agents. They helped me think about ways to shape this book when I really needed help. Thanks also to Derek Johns, Sarah Thickett, and Georgina Carrigan at AP Watt/United Agents; Casey Blue James, Laura Perciasepe, and Elizabeth Hohenadel at Riverhead; Ira Glass, Julie Snyder, and Brian Reed at *This American Life*; Jim Nelson and Brendan Vaughan at *GQ*; Ashley Cataldo at the American Antiquarian Society; Toni Massaro at the University of Arizona; Dan Kahan at Yale; and Sarah Vowell, Jonathan Wakeham, Starlee Kine, Fenton Bailey, Geoff Lloyd, Emma-Lee Moss, Mike McCarthy, Marc Maron,

Tim Minchin, Daniel and Paula Ronson, Leslie Hobbs, Brian Daniels, Barbara Ehrenreich, Marty Sheehan, and Camilla Elworthy.

My biggest thanks go to my interviewees, especially Jonah Lehrer, Justine Sacco, Lindsey Stone, Hank, Adria Richards, and Raquel. These people had never before spoken to a journalist about what had happened to them. I was asking them to relive for me some of the most traumatic moments of their lives. Some of them took a lot of persuading, and I hope they think it was worthwhile.